Editor:
Paul Gardner

Editor in Chief:
Sharon Coan, M.S. Ed.

Art Director:
Elayne Roberts

Associate Designer:
Denise Bauer

Production Manager:
Phil Garcia

Imaging:
James Edward Grace

Trademarks:
Trademarked names and graphics appear throughout this book. Instead of listing every firm and entity which owns the trademarks or inserting a trademark symbol with each mention of a trademarked name, the publisher avers that it is using the names and graphics only for editorial purposes and to the benefit of the trademarked owner with no intention of infringing upon that trademark.

Publishers:
Rachelle Cracchiolo, M.S. Ed.
Mary Dupuy Smith, M.S. Ed.

The Print Shop®
for
Terrified Teachers

Authors:

Marsha Lifter and Marian Adams

Teacher Created Materials, Inc.
6421 Industry Way
Westminster, CA 92683
ISBN-1-57690-189-0

©1998 Teacher Created Materials, Inc.
Made in U.S.A.

TABLE OF CONTENTS

TABLE OF CONTENTS *(cont.)*

INTRODUCTION

It seems that nearly everyone has *The Print Shop* in some form at school or at home. *The Print Shop* published by Brøderbund was one of the first production tools used in schools. When it was first published, teachers produced banners and greeting cards by the bundle for every occasion. How excited teachers and students were to see the banners and greeting cards spew forth from the printer! Then when color ribbons became available for the early printers, the excitement grew even stronger. Name an occasion, and a banner or card was produced. Teachers were very excited about the graphics that were available and how easily they could be placed into compositions.

Now, a new group of *The Print Shops*, also published by Brøderbund, have appeared on the scene. These programs are for both the Macintosh and the Windows environments. With these new *Print Shop* programs, there is an even broader array of graphics and printing capabilities.

The Print Shop for Terrified Teachers is designed to walk you through all of the wonderful projects that you can easily create with your computer. All of the descriptions for step-by-step procedures are fully illustrated. The book is organized into the following categories:

The Print Shop Walkthroughs

Step-by-step directions for using *The Print Shop Deluxe* and *The Print Shop Companion* are given. With the walkthrough you will be creating the following projects:

- Greeting cards
- Signs and posters
- Banners
- Certificates
- Letterhead
- Envelopes
- Postcards
- Business cards
- Smart graphics
- Graphics exporter
- Calendars

Press Writer Walk Through

Step-by-step directions for *The Print Shop PressWriter* are supplied.

Teacher Projects

There are step-by-step directions for creating classroom materials:

- Big and little books
- Letterheads and notepads
- Large posters
- Tent markers
- Personalized message pads
- Educator business cards
- Game cards and flash cards
- Classroom banners
- Classroom logs

Student Projects

There are step-by-step directions for student projects for lower, middle, and upper grades. Duplicate the instructions for the step-by-step activities, place them next to the computer, and let your students enjoy and expand. As students follow the directions, they will learn the various components of the program as well as important technology skills. Find a complete list of projects on page 163.

Use *The Print Shop* for making transparencies to use with the overhead projector. Use *The Print Shop* for making templates for students to use in the classroom. Allow yourself to become creative as you learn the program. You will be amazed at the creativity waiting to jump out through your fingers.

Enjoy!

SPECIAL NOTES FOR WINDOWS USERS

The Print Shop series of programs is published in both Macintosh and Windows versions. The directions in *The Print Shop for Terrified Teachers* were written for use both on Macintosh and Windows machines. Basically, the directions in this book will work on a Windows machine with a few small additions. There are also some features unique to the Windows version. These will be marked with an asterisk *.

Windows: Starting New Projects

When you open a new project from the Select a Project dialog box, you are given two choices:

- Customize a Ready Made
- Start from Scratch

The Customize a Ready Made selection presents a layout with graphics that can be modified to suit your needs. The Start from Scratch option presents you with a blank page on which to create layouts and graphics.

Spell Check, Thesaurus, and Quotes and Verses

*Spell Check, Thesaurus, and Quotes and Verses are options which can be accessed from the File menu when you are using the Text Block.

Spell Check: Click Spell Check to check the entire contents of an Edit dialog box for misspelled or unfamiliar words. If an unfamiliar word is found:

- Replace With field–you can select a word from the Alternatives list to place in this field.
- Alternatives field–displays a list of suggested alternate words.
- Not Found field–displays the word not found.

SPECIAL NOTES FOR WINDOWS
USERS *(cont.)*

- Ignore–ignores a word and continues spell checking the rest of the text.
- Replace–click to accept the word in the Replace With field.
- Add–adds a word to the Spell Check dictionary.

*Thesaurus: Search for synonyms for a currently highlighted word from within the Edit Text Block, Edit Word Balloon, or Edit Headline Text dialog boxes:

- Searched For field–displays the word being searched for in the thesaurus.
- Meanings field–displays a list of the meanings for the word being searched for.
- Replace With Synonym field–type a word or select a word from the Meanings list to replace the word in the Searched For field.
- Search–finds the synonym for the word displayed in the Replace With Synonym field.
- Previous–displays the previously searched for word.
- Replace–replaces the word in the Searched For field with the contents of the Replaced With Synonym field and closes the Thesaurus dialog box.

*Quotes and Verses Browser: Over 1,000 quotes and verses that can be incorporated into projects exist in the Windows version. In Edit Text or Edit Word Balloon Text dialog box, you can click on the Quotes and Verses button to easily add poetry, proverbs, humor, holiday greetings, and birthday facts to your projects.

- Search button–searches for specific quotes and verses based on a keyword or keywords.
- Keywords field–type in keywords.
- Add Project Text button–adds text from the project to the Keywords field.
- Category Keywords button–takes you to the Keywords dialog box where you can choose from a list of search subjects.
- Search Preferences button– search for all words in the Keywords box individually or search for all words as they appear together.

ONLINE GREETING CARDS AND THE INTERNET CONNECTION

You can create a unique online greeting with text and graphics and send it to someone over the Internet. Your greeting appears as an attachment in the e-mail of the person receiving the message. You must be connected to the Internet in order send the greeting. The recipient must be able to view JPEG image files.

In addition, Brøderbund provides registered *The Print Shop* users technical support and lots of free graphics at their *The Print Shop* Connection Web site. You can access it at

http://www.printshop.com/

THE PRINT SHOP IDEA GUIDE

There are three different graphic project themes in the Idea Guide: Party Ideas, Gift Ideas, and Holiday Ideas.

When you select one of these project themes, you are presented with four different projects with that theme:

- Party Ideas, Invitation, Table Runner, Place Card, and Game Poster.
- Gift Ideas, Gift Label, Gift Certificate, Money Envelope, and Recipe Card.
- Holiday Ideas, Greeting Card, Ornament, Paper Chain, and Count Down (a calendar).

The Idea Guide is stored on *The Print Shop Ensemble III* CD. To open the *Ensemble* Idea Guide in Windows 95:

- Insert the CD into you CD-ROM drive.
- Click start.
- Point to Programs—*The Print Shop*.
- Click *Ensemble* Idea Guide Icon.

The step-by-step instructions for each of these project ideas are presented using verbal instructions and animation. To print a copy of the instructions:

- Click How to (the *Ensemble* Idea Guide Help section opens with the project areas listed).
- Click Party Ideas.
- Click Invitation.
- Click File menu.
- Select Print Topic.

The instructions for the party invitation are printed.

THE TOOLS AND THE TOOL PALETTE

Teacher Note: Duplicate these pages, glue them onto file folders, laminate them, and display them in the computer area for student reference.

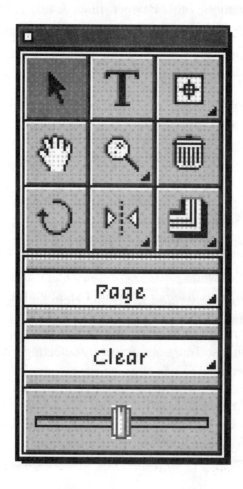

THE TOOLS AND THE TOOL PALETTE *(cont.)*

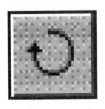

Rotate Tool

The Rotate Tool lets you rotate objects that have been selected. Click on a corner of the selected object and drag in either a clockwise or counterclockwise direction until the object is in the position in which you want it. If you want to rotate the object by a specific number of degrees, you can do it by selecting rotate from the Object menu and type or select the specific rotation that you want.

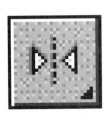

Flip Tool

The Flip Tool lets you flip a selected graphic object (except borders and mini-borders) *horizontally, vertically* or *both.* When you select this tool, a menu appears. Choose Horizontal, Vertical, or Both. You can also *flip* an object by selecting Flip from the Object menu.

Frame Tool

The Frame Tool lets you place a frame around a selected object. When you select this tool, a menu appears. The choices are *None, Thin Line, Thick Line, Double Line,* or *Drop Shadow.* The current setting of the selected object is shown by a check mark. If a number of objects with different frame settings are selected, no check mark will appear. You can also frame an object by selecting *Frame* from the Object menu.

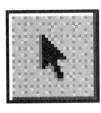

Pointer Tool

The Pointer Tool lets you select, move, and resize objects. To select an object, click on it. Handles appear at the corners of the object. This tells you that the object is selected.

THE TOOLS AND THE TOOL PALETTE *(cont.)*

To select additional objects, hold down the shift key while you click on the additional objects. You can change the size of the selected object by holding the mouse arrow down on one of the handles and moving the handle in or out to change the size. You move the object by holding down the mouse arrow in the center and moving the object to where you want it placed. Borders and backdrops cannot be resized.

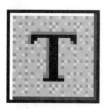

Text Tool

The Text Tool lets you create text blocks, enter text, and select text to edit. To create a new text block, put the text cursor where you want the upper-left corner of the text block to be placed and drag diagonally to create a text box. You can now enter text in the block. If you want to change the font, size, style, justification and/or placement, highlight the text and use the Text menu to make the changes. To change the color of the text, use the Color Bar on the Tool Palette.

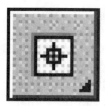

New Object Tool

The New Object Tool lets you add new objects to your projects.

- Square Graphic
- Row Graphic
- Column Graphic
- Text Block
- Headline
- Horizontal Ruled Line
- Vertical ruled Line
- Mini Border
- Border

THE TOOLS AND THE TOOL PALETTE *(cont.)*

Hold down your mouse arrow on the New Object Tool and move your mouse to the choice you want to select. Release the mouse button and the Placeholder for the choice appears on your screen. Move the Placeholder by clicking and dragging it to where you want it to beplaced. Change the size by clicking and dragging one of the handles. To select a graphic or enter text, double-click on the Placeholder.

Hand Tool

The Hand Tool lets you move your project around within the window. To use the Hand Tool, put the hand on your project and drag.

View Tool

The View Tool lets you change your view of the project. Select this tool and a menu will appear:

- Zoom In
- Zoom Out
- Fit in Window—the default for most projects, shows your project in a size that fits in the document window of your monitor
- Actual Size—shows the project at the size it is when printed out
- 25%—one quarter actual size
- 50%—one half actual size
- 150%—one and a half times actual size
- 200%—twice actual size

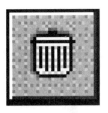

Delete Tool

The Delete Tool lets you delete a selected object. If you change your mind and want the deleted object back, select Undo from the Edit menu.

THE TOOLS AND THE TOOL PALETTE *(cont.)*

Color Control Panel

You can choose colors for various parts of the design by choosing items in the Color Control Panel. Click on the object you want to color using the Pointer tool. Click on the Item Selector and choose an area to color from the menu that appears:

- Object (or Text)
- Behind the Object (or Text)
- Frame
- Backdrop
- Page

The current color for the selected location is shown in the Color Bar. Multi-colored objects are represented by three color splashes or the words "multi-colored." If the multi-colored objects are selected, they can not be changed. If the item selected can be colored, click on the Color Bar and move to the color that you want to choose.

THE PRINT SHOP WALK THROUGH INDEX

The Print Shop Walkthrough Index

The Print Shop Deluxe Components

The Print Shop Companion Components

USING THE GREETING CARD PROJECT

The Greeting Card project category allows you to make four different designs of greeting cards:

- Side fold
- Side fold spread
- Top fold
- Top fold spread

For this walkthrough, we will make a thank you card.

1. From the main menu, select Greeting Card. On the following screen, select the card style that you want. Choose top fold for this project.

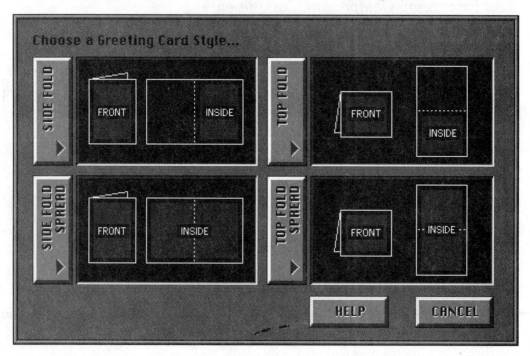

2. On the next screen, you can select a Landscape Backdrop.

3. For this sample, we chose Blank Page. Click OK.

4. The next screen allows you to select a layout. For this sample, choose Layout 24. Click OK.

5. Double-click on the exclamation mark, and you are taken to the Headline Text box. Key in your headline. Choose a shape from the shape menu by holding down the arrow and selecting a shape.

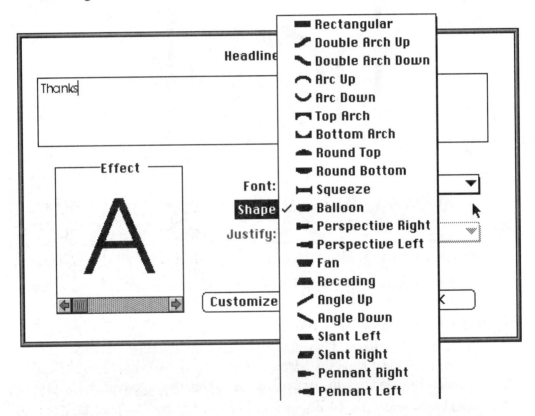

6. For this example, we chose Balloon. Click OK.

7. To add a border, double-click on the greyed out Border and choose from the Border Menu. If the border is not greyed out, select Object from the Menu Bar and choose Border.

8. Click OK, and you have your card front on the screen. Notice in the lower left corner it shows where on the card you are working.

9. You can go to the inside of the card in two different ways.

  • Select Project from the Menu Bar and choose Inside Card.

  • Select the arrow at the bottom left corner of the screen, hold it down, and move it to Inside Card.

10. On the inside of the card, we chose No Layout. To add a graphic to the card, select Object from the Menu Bar and choose Add and then Square Graphic. Double click the graphic holder to choose a graphic.

11. To add text, select the T from the Tool Palette and make a text box. Key in your text. If the text is too large for the area, highlight it and choose Size from the Text menu on the Menu Bar. Then choose a size.

12. Another way to add text is to select Object from the Menu bar and choose Text Block. This puts a text block in the middle of your page. You can enlarge it by moving the handles. Double-click on the "T" and type your text.

Thanks for showing us the new books in the library. We especially liked the books about space.
Room 17

13. Select Back of Card from the Project Menu and then choose a layout or choose No Layout.

14. For this project, we chose Landscape Layout 8 to have a place for a graphic and text.

15. Save and Print your card.

Created by Room 17 with our new computer

USING THE SIGN PROJECT

Making a "Back to School Night" Poster Without Graphics

The Sign Project allows you to make posters, big books, regular sized books, announcements, general signage, tent signs, etc.

For this walkthrough, we are going to make a poster advertising "Back to School Night."

We will be using a predesigned layout to make a Sign/Poster.

1. Open Sign from the main menu by clicking on the word Sign. This takes you to a Sign Orientation screen where you can choose the Tall or Wide format.

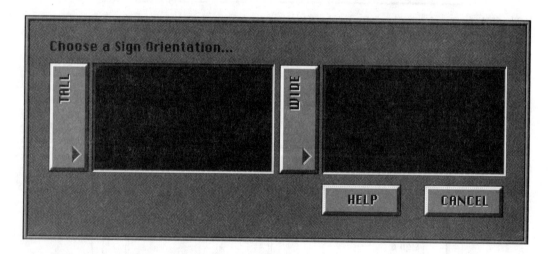

2. Choose the Tall orientation.

3. On the next screen, you can choose the Portrait Backdrop for your poster. For this particular project, choose Blank Page. Click OK.

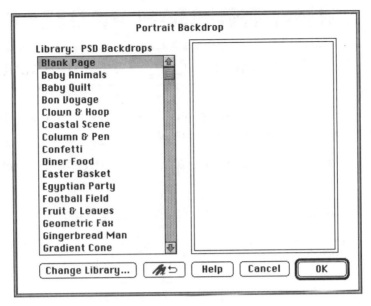

4. At the next screen you can choose an interesting layout. These layouts indicate where the graphics and text are placed. These layouts are arranged in various combinations and configurations designed to work well with the backdrop of your choice. You can choose No Layout or one of the predesigned layouts. For this project, we chose a predesigned layout.

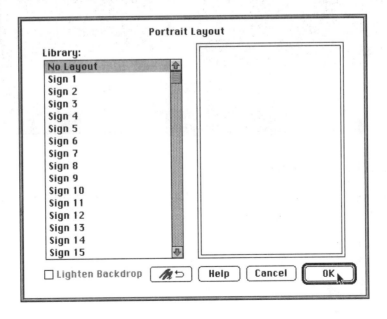

5. Select Sign 29 for this activity and click OK.

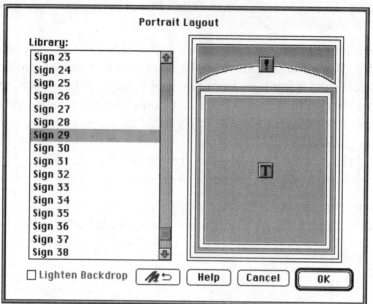

6. The top section is marked with an exclamation mark and is the headline.
   The bottom section is marked with a "T," and that marks the area for the
   text.

7. To write the headline, double-click on the exclamation mark. You are now
   presented with a text box in which you enter the text that you want for the
   headline. For this activity, key in Come Back to School and click OK. You
   can change font and shape and also Customize from this screen.

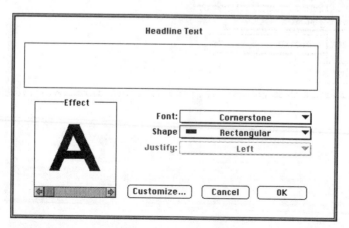

8. It's time to write the text for the poster now. Double-click on the "T" area in the middle of the screen and compose your text. You will notice that the text is centered and moves over automatically.

9. If you want to place a small graphic in the corner of the sign, select Object from the Menu Bar and move to Add and over to Square Graphic. You can also select the Object icon from the Tool Palette. When this is selected, you are presented with graphic choices. Choose one that is appropriate. When it appears on the screen, move the graphic to where you want it placed by placing the mouse arrow in the center of the graphic and holding down the mouse button. Move the graphic. To change the size of the graphic, put the mouse arrow on one of the handles and move it in or out.

10. To place a border on the poster, double-click on the border and choose from the Border menu. To see the various choices, click once on a border and it shows in the preview area. When you find one that you like, click OK to place.

11. To print, select Print from the File menu. This prints one poster on a page. If you want a larger print, select More Options from the Print dialog box and then choose the size desired.

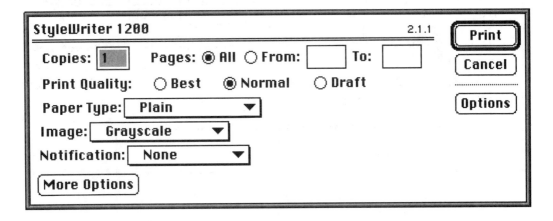

Making a Poetry Poster with Graphics

1. Select the Sign project and the Wide Orientation.

2. Choose Blank Page and click OK.

3. Choose No Layout and click OK.

4. To write the poem title, select Object and choose the Headline Text. Move the Headline to the top of the page. Double-click and key in the text.

5. To change the shape and font of the headline, use the Shape and Font menus as found on the screen.

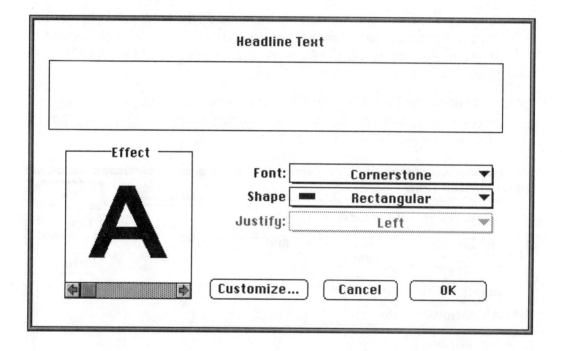

6. When you find the shape of the headline that suits your needs, click OK.

7. Now it is time to key in the text. Select Text Block from the Object menu on the Menu Bar. Enlarge the text block by moving the mouse arrow to a handle and pull out on both sides.

8. Add a graphic to the poster by selecting Square Graphic from the Object menu. When the graphics are listed, and you don't see one that is appropriate, select Change Library from the bottom of the screen. The dialog box asks you where the Library is located. Click to change to the desktop and click on the hard drive if that is where your libraries are located. You can use the book that accompanies *The Print Shop* programs to choose your graphics before working at the computer.

StyleWriter 1200	2.1.1	Print

Copies: [1]   Pages: ◉ All ○ From: [ ]   To: [ ]   [Cancel]

Print Quality: ○ Best   ◉ Normal   ○ Draft

Paper Type: [Plain   ▼]   [Options]

Image: [Grayscale   ▼]

Notification: [None   ▼]

[More Options]

9. To print a larger poster, from the Print dialog menu, select More Options. Place your mouse on the arrow next to Project Size and choose a larger size.

Print Mode: ☐ Coloring Book

Project Size: [1x1 ▼]

Print Area Adjustment: [Default   ▼]

☐ Two Color Dither – For ImageWriter II With Color Ribbon

☐ Save Printer Selection   [Cancel]   [OK]

Where Go the Boats ?

Dark brown is the river,
Golden is the sand,
It flows along forever,
With trees on either
hand.
Green leaves a floating.
Castles of the foam,
Boats of mine a-boating--
Where will they come
home.

by
Rober Louis Stevenson

I Am a Ghost Who's Lost His Boo

by Bert Prelutsky

I am a ghost who's lost his boo,
my boo is gone from me,
and I'm without a single clue
to where my boo might be.
It makes me mope, it makes me pout,
it almost makes me moan,
a ghost without a boo to call his own.

My boo was piercing, fierce, and loud,
I used to strut and boast,
for I was positively proud
to be a gruesome ghost.
But now that I'm without a boo,
I find it rather weird,
there's little for a ghost to do
whose boo has disappeared.

Paul Revere's Ride

Henry Wadsworth Longfellow

Listen my children and you shall hear
Of the midnight ride of Paul Revere.
On the eighteenth of April in Seventy-five;
Hardly a man is now alive
Who remembers that famous day and year.
He said to his friend, "If the British march
By land and sea from town to tonight,
Hang a lantern aloft in the belfry arch
Of the North Church tower, as a signal light_

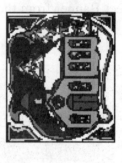

USING THE BANNER PROJECT

The Banner project makes banners in both horizontal and vertical modes. For this walkthrough, we will be making a banner to place over the class library center.

1. Select Banner from the main menu.

2. On the next screen choose Horizontal or Vertical.

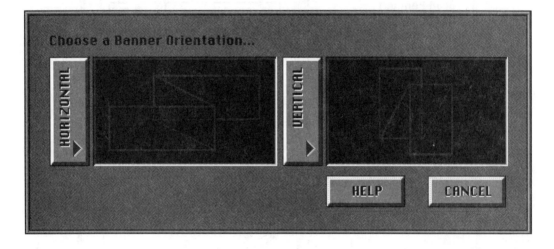

3. For this project we chose the Horizontal orientation.

4. On the next screen, choose a Backdrop or No Backdrop and click OK.

5. On the next screen, choose the layout you want or choose No Layout and click OK.

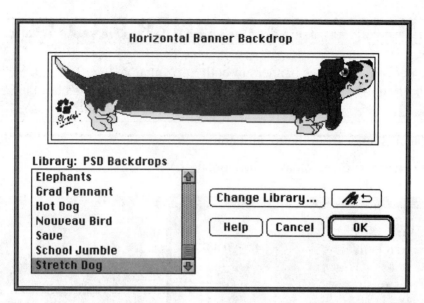

6. Double-click on the exclamation mark, and you will get a Banner Text screen.

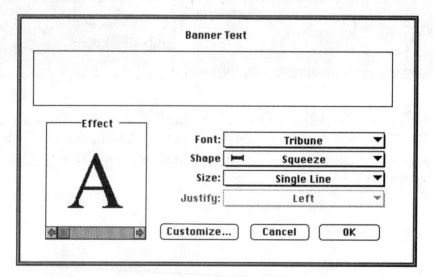

7. Write your text. You can modify the font and size by choosing Font and Size from the Banner Text menu.

8. If you decide to change the text, double-click on it, and you are taken back to the Banner Text menu.

9. Save and print.

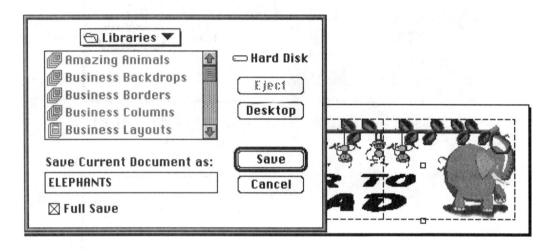

Note: *The Print Shop Deluxe* performs two kinds of saves: Full Saves and Fast Saves. Fast Saves will save the text but not graphics. Use Full Saves if you want your graphics saved with the text. It takes up more room on the hard drive but is highly recommended.

USING THE LETTERHEAD PROJECT

For this walkthrough we are making letterhead stationery for teacher use.

1. Open the Letterhead project from the main menu.

2. The next screen lets you choose either a Single Page (8.5 by 11 or letterhead size) or a Notepad size (5.5 x 8.5, printed 2 to a sheet).

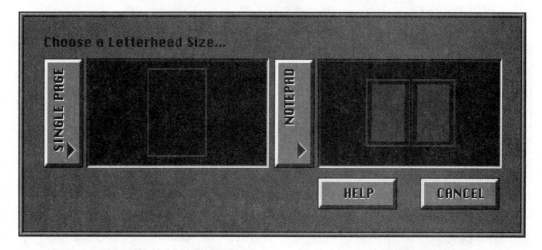

3. For this project, we chose Single Page. Now it is time to choose a Backdrop or Blank Page. For this walkthrough we chose Blank Page and then Layout #3.

4. Double-click on the Text Placeholder and key in your information. We used the teacher's name and the name of the school.

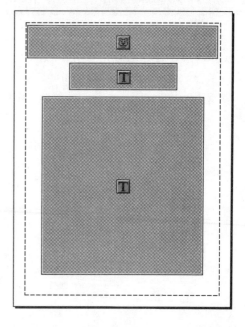

5. To modify the text entry, highlight the text by holding down the mouse arrow key and moving over the text. Select the Text menu from the Menu Bar and choose Text Settings. This allows you to change font, size, and style.

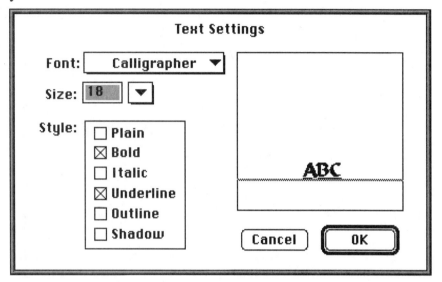

6. To add graphics to the top of the page, double-click in the Graphic Placeholder and find a graphic that you would like on the top of the page. To resize the graphic, place the mouse arrow at a handle and move in or out to resize the graphic.

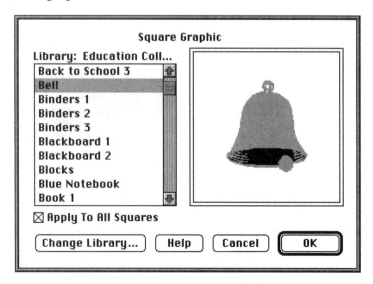

7. To add a border to the stationery, select Object from the Menu bar, select Add and then choose Borders. Choose the border you want and click OK to place it.

8. You can now double-click on the Text Placeholder to write a letter, or leave the area blank and it will print out with a blank space in which you can write your notes.

9. Save and print. Be sure to save your notepaper to use again and again.

Making Letterhead Using Column Graphics

1. When you choose the Layout, choose one that shows the placeholder for Column Graphics.

2. If you don't find a graphic you like, select Change Libraries and locate the appropriate graphic.

Making Letterhead and Modifying a Graphic Square

1. To rotate or flip the graphic, click on the rotate or Flip Tool in the Tool Palette.

    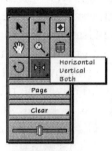

    • To flip the graphic, select the Flip Tool from the Tool Palette. Hold down the mouse button and choose one of the three selections given.

    • To rotate the object, select the Rotate Tool and the mouse arrow turns into a semicircle with an arrow at one end. Move the arrow to a corner of the highlighted graphic, hold down the mouse button, and move in whichever direction you want.

2. Double-click in the text box to write your message.

Making Letterhead with Shadowed and Framed Graphics

1. Choose a Layout that has Square Graphics in it. Double-click the Square Graphic placeholder and choose a graphic. To make a frame and/or a shadow, select the Frame Tool, hold down the mouse button and choose either frame or shadow. You must click on the graphic first to select it. That way the computer knows where to put the shadow or frame.

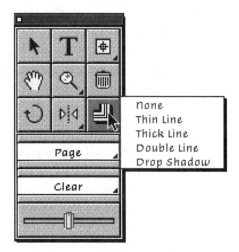

Making Letterhead and Changing Text Color

1. Choose your Layout and place your graphic.

2. Click once on the Text Placeholder to highlight it.

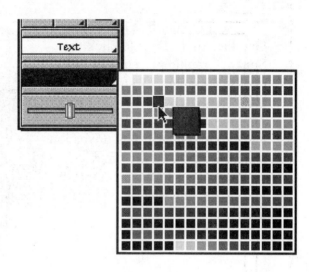

3. Notice that the Tool Palette shows Text because you highlighted the text. Notice also that it is black in the space underneath Text. To change the color of text from black to another color, hold down the mouse button and move to the right to select a color. The color box changes to your choice.

4. Double-click in the text placeholder and write your text.

HINTS:

- To edit text, you must have the mouse pointer showing. If not, click on the pointer tool in the tool palette. Double-click on the text you wish to edit. You can then move text and highlight text for further changes.

- If you accidentally delete text, you can bring it right back by selecting Undo from the Edit menu. THIS IS A VERY IMPORTANT THING TO KNOW. You can go one step back by using the Undo from the Edit menu.

Please join us:
Sept. 28 at 10:30
Tom's Apple Farm
Hwy. 136

We need your help to pick
apples for the apple pies we
are going to make.
Room 6

USING THE CALENDAR PROJECT

Making a Weekly Calendar

For this walkthrough we are making two different types of calendars: weekly and monthly.

1. Select Calendar from the main menu.

2. From the next screen, select a Calendar Type by clicking in the appropriate section.

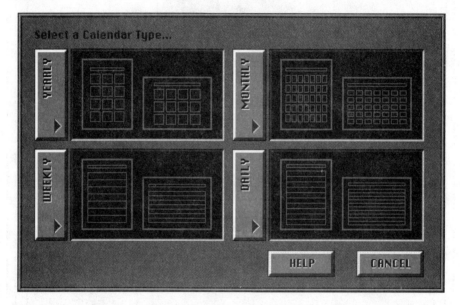

3. For this example, we chose Weekly.

4. On the next screen, you can choose the Orientation. The Tall orientation was chosen for this project.

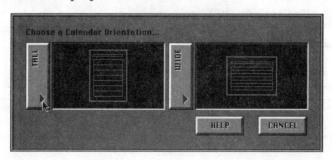

5. The next screen provides an area where you can customize the month and dates of your calendar. Enter this information and click OK.

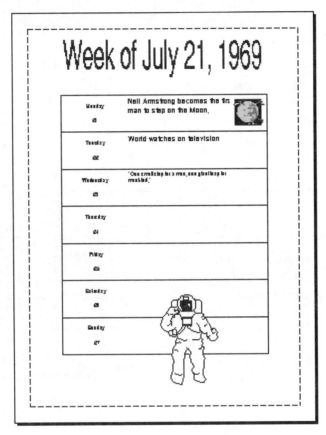

6. To add text to a specific day of the week, double-click in the date area.

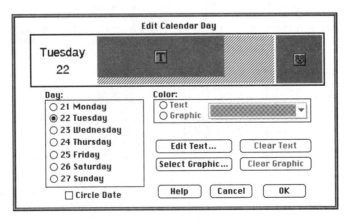

7. Select Edit Text and key in your text.

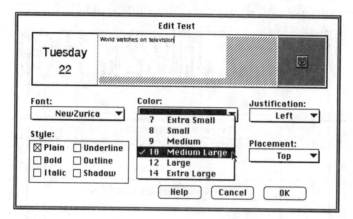

8. To change text size, hold down the arrow in the Size menu and choose a size. Click OK to choose. You can choose the color of the text by holding down the arrow in the Color menu and selecting a color.

9. To add a border, select Object and choose Add and then Border.

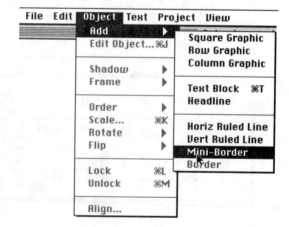

10. Save and Print your calendar.

Week of July 21, 1969

Monday 21	Neil Armstrong becomes the first man to step on the Moon.
Tuesday 22	World watches on television
Wednesday 23	"One small step for a man, one giant leap for mankind."
Thursday 24	
Friday 25	
Saturday 26	
Sunday 27	

Making a Monthly Calendar

1. Select Calendar from the main menu and choose the type of calendar. For this example, we chose Monthly and Wide for the orientation.

2. The next screen allows you to choose the month and year.

3. The calendar we are making shows the harvest schedule for fruits and vegetables. Choose Blank Page from the next menu, click OK, and choose the Layout from the next screen. You can choose a preformatted layout or choose to have no layout and place your graphics and text where you want them. For this project we chose Calendar 6. Click OK.

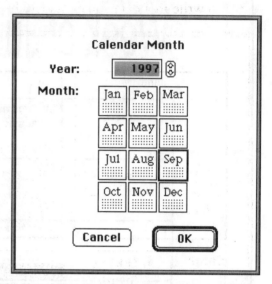

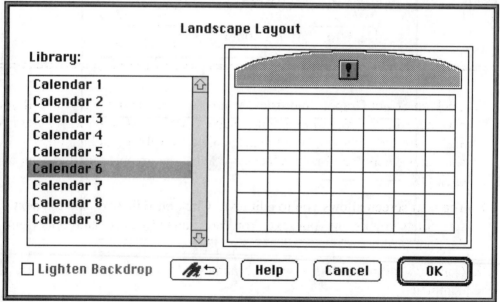

4. To change the look of the text, double-click and you are presented with the Headline Text choices where you can change font and headline shape.

5. To change the headline shape, hold down the arrow on the right and select another shape.

6. To write in a date square and add a graphic, double-click in the date box.

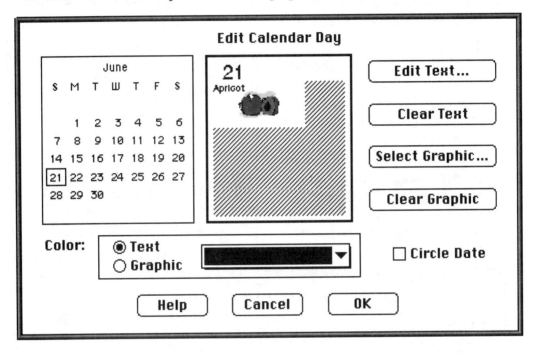

7. Click on Select Graphic and from the next screen, choose a graphic. If you have added *The Print Shop* graphics such as those that come with *The Print Shop Ensemble*, you will want to select Change Library and tell the computer where the library is located. Select the graphic that you want and click OK.

8. The next screen allows you to edit text. Click on Edit Text, and the next screen lets you key in your text. You can change font size and fonts from the Font menu.

9. Continue editing each date with a graphic and text until your calendar is complete.

10. To add more text to the calendar, select Object, select Add, and move to Text Block. Move the text block to where you want it. Double-click on the "T" and start typing. To change the font and size, double-click on the text and you get highlighting. Move the highlighting to highlight the words; select Text from the Menu Bar and for Font, Style, or Size. Change as you wish. Click outside of the box to see how it looks. If you want to make any other changes to the text, double-click on the text and repeat the instructions from above.

11. Save and print your calendar.

EXPORTING GRAPHICS FROM THE PRINT SHOP

The Exporting Graphics project lets you export graphics from *The Print Shop* and then import them into another program. You can export *The Print Shop Deluxe*, *Companion* and compatible Graphics Collections and folios in three different file formats: EPSF (Encapsulated PostScript Format), PICT, and AI (Adobe Illustrator).

1. Open the folder with the Exporter and double-click on the Exporter icon.

Exporter

The next screen is the title screen for the Exporter. Click OK, and you can now select a graphic using the Exporter's graphic selection window.

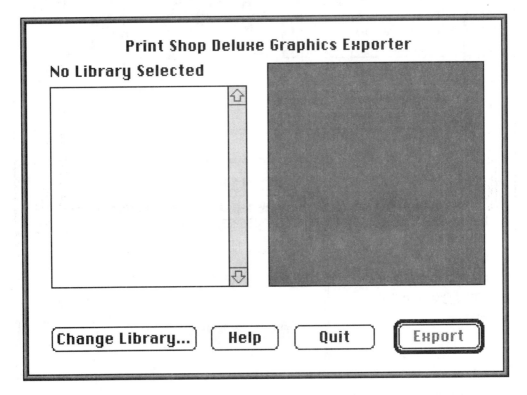

2. You now need to select the graphic that you want to export. To do this, you first have to select the Graphics Library where the graphic is located. Click on the Change Library button in the Graphics selection dialog box. Locate the library file containing the graphic you want by double-clicking on "Libraries." Highlight the library name and click Open or double-click on the library name.

3. A list of graphics in that library appears on the left. Click on the graphic you want.

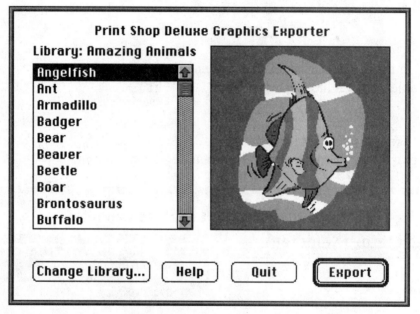

4. Click on the Export button and a Save Dialog Box appears. Click on the button next to the format in which you want it saved.

5. If you want it saved on your hard drive, you need to select Desktop and then your hard drive. If you have a specific folder into which you save your graphics, select that folder and then select Save.

6. When you are ready to import the graphic into another document, you just need to locate it where it is saved and import it into your document.

Made by importing a graphic from Print Shop into Kid Pix.

USING THE CERTIFICATE PROJECT

Designing a Certificate from Scratch

The Print Shop allows you to create your own individualized certificate or if you so desire, select a Ready Made certificate which you can modify. This walk-through is for the creation of a "from scratch" certificate.

1. Windows: Open the Certificate project from the main menu. Macintosh: Open *The Print Shop Companion* and select Certificate.

2. From the Certificate Orientation screen select either Wide or Tall. For this walk-through, we chose Wide.

3. The Backdrop dialog screen appears. The left area lists the names of pre-made backdrops. To preview them click on a name and it will preview in the display area. For this project, we selected Blank Page. Click OK.

4. Now it is time to select the layout for the certificate from the Landscape Layout screen. The layout screens have placeholders for the various elements of the design. Click on the different layouts and preview them in the display area. For this project we chose Certificate 6. Click OK after you have chosen your layout.

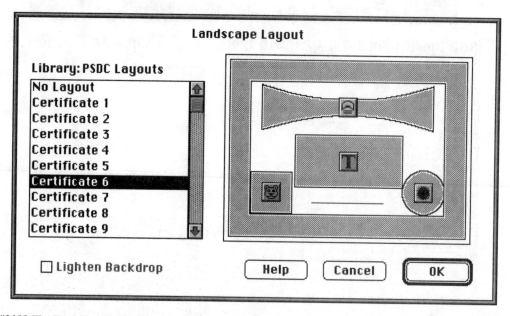

5. Now comes the fun part. You actually design your own certificate.

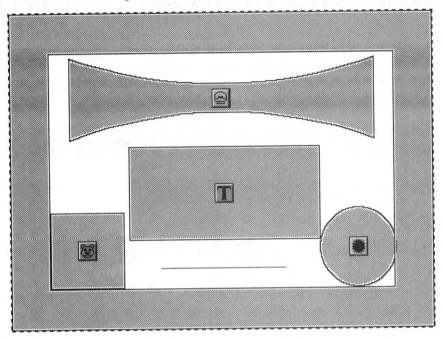

6. Double-click on the Title Block. The next screen lets you design the Title Block.

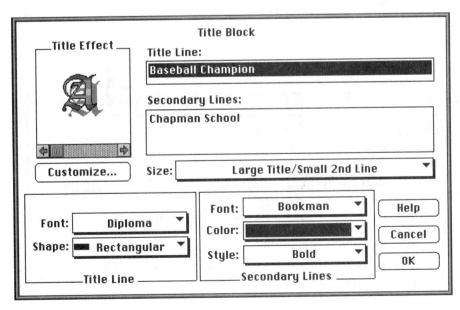

Key in your title. Look in the lower left-hand corner where there are two options for the title line. You can change the font or the shape of the title. If you hold down the arrow next to the font name, you will be presented with many fonts from which to choose.

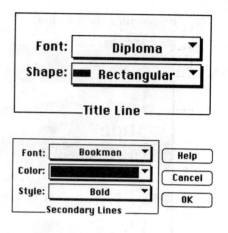

If you want to change anything about the text you entered, you must highlight the text first. Key in the secondary line and modify it by using the choices in the Secondary Lines box in the lower right-hand corner.

7. You can also make changes through the Title Effect box. Clicking on the right or left arrows moves you through a series of font effect choices. Clicking on the Customize box leads to a Custom Effect dialog box.

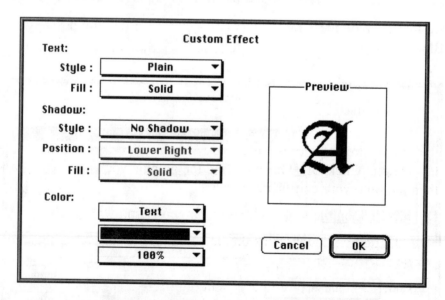

8. To add text, double-click on the text placeholder. If the font is too small, select Text from the menu and choose Size. You are then given a size menu from which to choose the size you want.

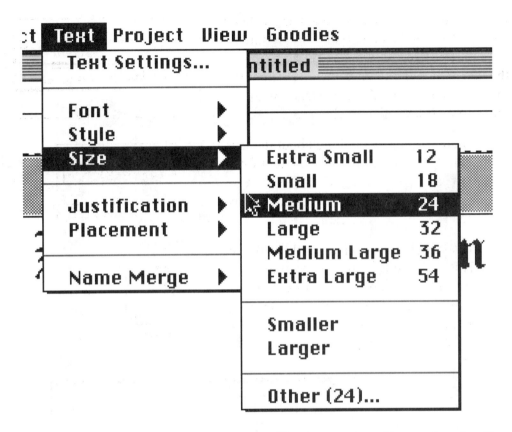

For this project, we chose Medium Large. Key in you text. Remember that if you want to change the text, you must highlight the text first.

9. To add a graphic, double-click on the graphic placeholder. The graphic in the sample project is from the Square Graphic, Sports and Games 1, Collection. Click OK when you find the graphic you want. The graphic is then put onto your certificate.

10. Double-click on the seal to choose your center and seal edge.

11. To add a border, double-click on the border and select an appropriate border for your certificate.

12. To type in a name beneath the signature line, double-click on the signature line, and you are then taken to the Edit Signature screen. Proceed from there to edit your name. (Refer to Using a Ready Made Certificate section of this book for illustrations of the applicable screens.)

USING READY MADE CERTIFICATES

The Certificate project contains many Ready Made certificates where all you do is double-click on an area you want to personalize, make those changes, and print.

1. *Windows:* Open the Certificate project from the main menu. *Macintosh:* Open *The Print Shop Companion* and select Certificate.

2. We chose Ready Made for this particular activity. Click on Ready Made, and you are presented with a list of ready made certificates. For this walkthrough, we chose Student. Of course, we need to customize the certificate to meet our classroom needs.

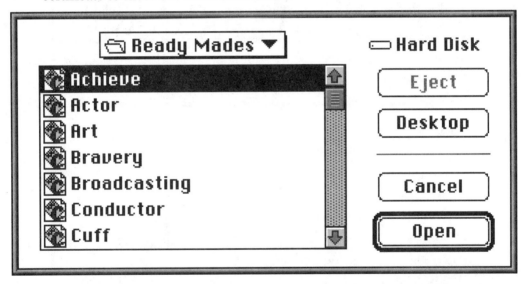

3. Double-click on the student name. This takes you to a Headline Text dialog box. Highlight the name and press delete. Key in the name you want. From this dialog box you can also choose font and style.

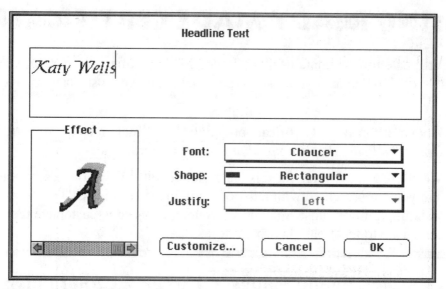

4. To further customize the name by adding color and effects, click on the Customize button in the lower left corner.

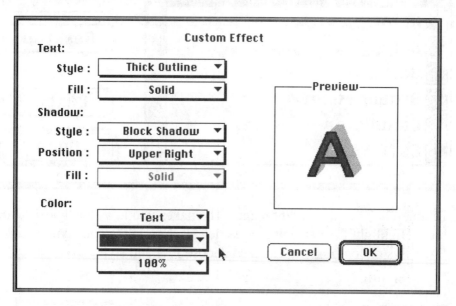

5. Choose a color from the Color menu. The preview shows how it will look. Click OK, and you are taken back to the certificate with the change made.

6. To edit the seal double-click on it, and you are taken to a seal dialog box. In this box, you can choose to edit the center or the edge of the seal along with adding text and changing font and color. For this project, we chose to edit the edge.

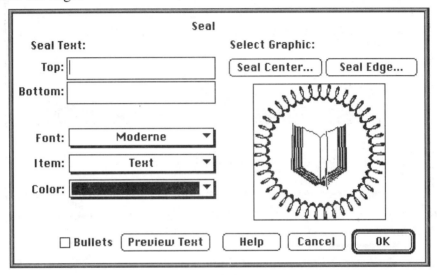

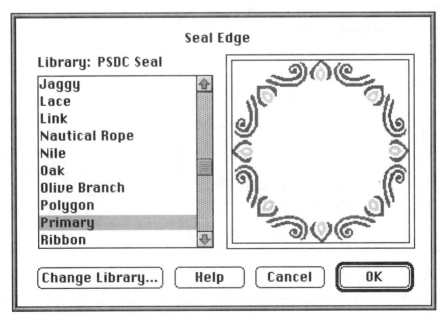

7. To edit the signature double-click in the signature area, and you are presented with an Edit Signature dialog box.

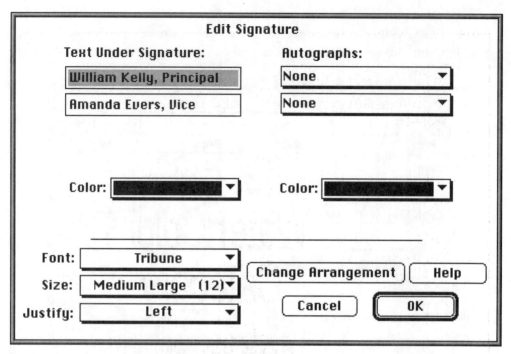

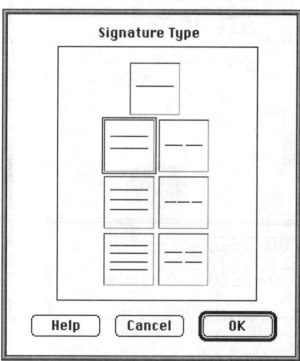

8. To change the number of signatures or their arrangement, choose Change Arrangement from the Edit Signature. Box and the Signature type box appears. Here you can select the arrangement and number of signatures. Click OK until you are back to the certificate.

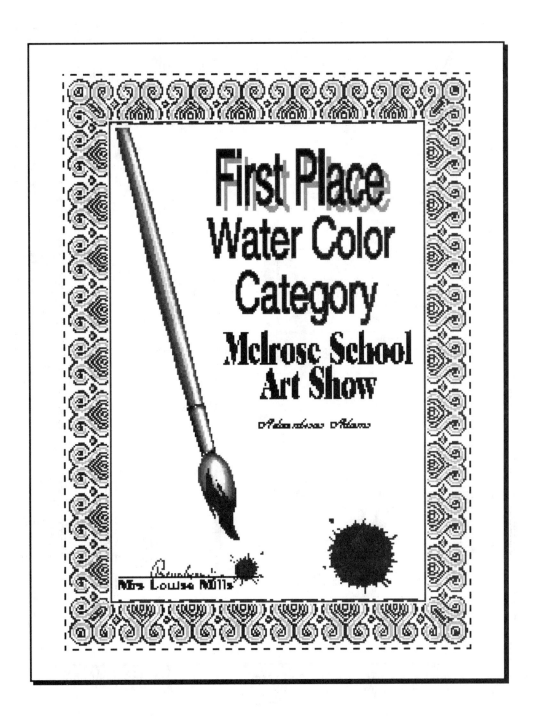

USING THE BUSINESS CARD PROJECT

The Business Card project can be used for making business cards as well as game cards and other items.

For this walkthrough we will make some amuzing business cards.

1. *Windows:* Open the Business Cards project from the main menu.
   Macintosh: Open *The Print Shop Companion* and select Business Cards.

2. The next screen lets you select a card orientation. For this project, we chose Wide.

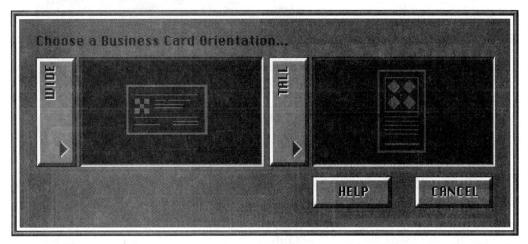

3. The next screen is where you choose a Landscape Backdrop. For this project we chose to Change Library and then chose the Graphics Plus Backdrops Library on the hard drive. We selected Witch's Deco.

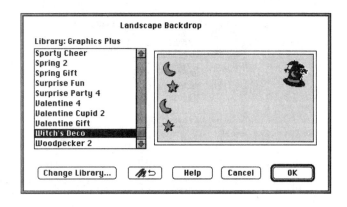

4. At the next screen you can choose the layout for your card. We chose Witch's Deco 2. You can also Lighten the Backdrop from this screen. Click OK, and you are ready to write your text. Double-click on the Text box and write your text.

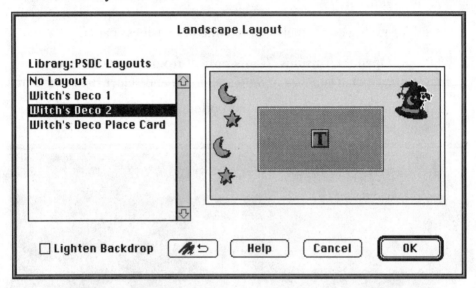

5. Now it is time to print your business card. Select Print from the File menu. A Print dialog box appears on the screen. You can choose the number of copies from this menu before you print. It prints 10 to a page automatically in the horizontal orientation. If you want crop marks to guide you in cutting the cards, select More Options from the print menu and check the box next to Crop Marks.

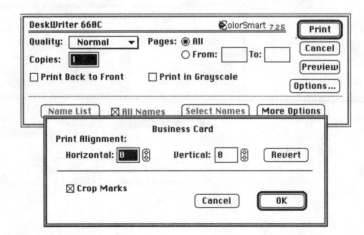

Project Examples

Wanda Witch
Professional Witch

Have broom will travel

1 800 Call Boo

USING THE POSTCARD PROJECT

The Postcard project has many creative uses for the classroom.

For this walk-through, we are going to make a postcard for the Thanksgiving holiday.

1. Windows: Open the Postcard project from the main menu. Macintosh: Open *The Print Shop Companion* and select Postcards.

2. On the next screen, you have a choice of Post Card Orientation.

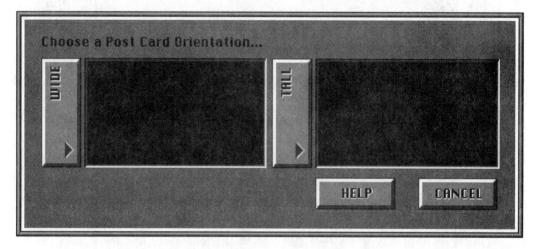

3. For this project we chose Wide.

4. The next screen allows you to Add a Backdrop. You can also change libraries from this screen. For this project, we chose Pilgrim from the PSD Library.

5. To add text to the front of the card, select Object from the menu bar and choose Add and then Text Block. When the text block appears, you can then size it by moving the handles out or in to the size desired or move the whole box by putting the mouse arrow in the middle of the box and moving your mouse. When ready, double-click on the text box and write your text.

6. If you want to add another graphic to the front of the card, select Object from the menu bar and choose Add and then Square Graphic. You can also move your graphic to where you want it placed.

7. Now you are ready to design the back side of the postcard. There are two ways to get to the back of the card: hold down the arrow at the lower left corner of the screen and move to Back of Post Card or select Project from the menu bar and choose Back of Postcard.

8. Choose a layout from the dialog box. For this project we chose Layout 2.

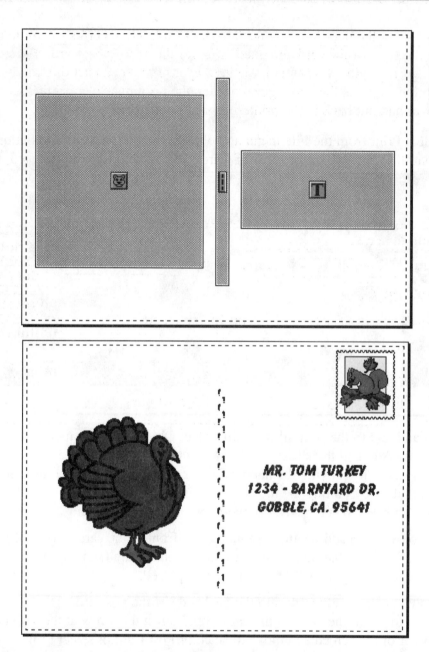

9. Double-click on the Square Graphic placeholder and choose a graphic. To put a stamp in the normal stamp area, select Object and Square Graphic. Place it in the stamp area. Stamps are found in the PDC Stamps Square Graphics library. Double-click on the text area to write in the address.

When you print the postcard, you need to run it through the printer two times, once for the front of the card and once more for the back of the card. Before you use the cardstock, do a trial run on regular paper. Printers all act differently. On the HP printer we use the paper goes through the printing cycle and then is turned over and put back in the printer to print on the back.

10. Select Print from the File menu and click at the bottom the radio button in front of Front of Card or Back of Card. When the postcard is printed, there is a cross-hair guide in the middle which aids you in cutting the cards apart.

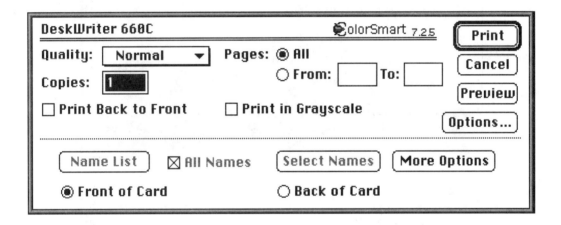

Postcard Examples

USING THE SMART GRAPHICS PROJECT

Smart Graphics allows the user to customize letters and numbers to use wherever a Square Graphic is called for. The graphics are saved in their own folder which can be accessed whenever placing a Square Graphic within any project.

1. Windows: Open the Smart Graphics project from the main menu.
   Macintosh: Open *The Print Shop Companion* and select Smart Graphics.

2. From the main menu, select Smart Graphics.

3. The next screen presents a choice of Initial Caps, Numbers or Timepieces.

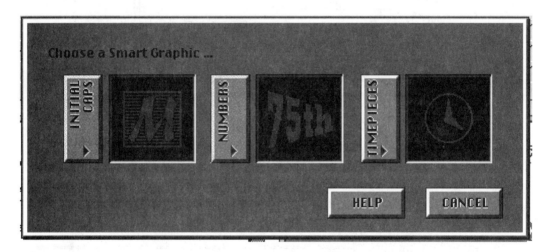

Option 1: Designing an Initial Cap for Use in Projects

1. After selecting Initial Cap you are presented with the Initial Cap screen where you can change font, type, shape, style, position, or color. Enter the letter you want in the upper left-hand box next to the word "Letter."

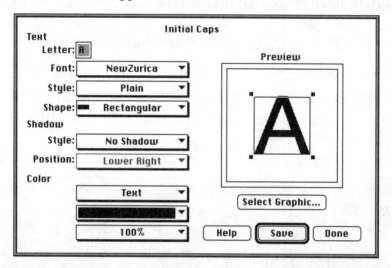

2. From this menu choose a font and a style that you like. Now choose a shape and color.

3. To select a graphic to surround the letter, click Select Graphic. From this screen you can select specifically designed graphics for the initial caps. Click OK and then click Done to return to a screen where the graphic can be saved.

4. A dialog box appears that asks if you want to save the graphic. If you click yes, you are taken to a screen where the items saved in the User Squares folder are listed. Type in a name for your graphic and click Save.

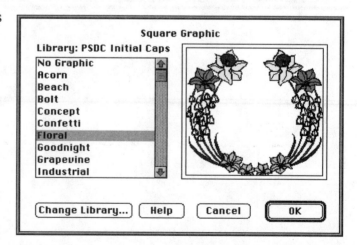

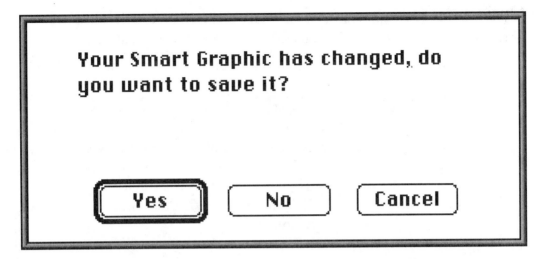

5. Your graphic is saved and is ready to use wherever a Square Graphic is needed.

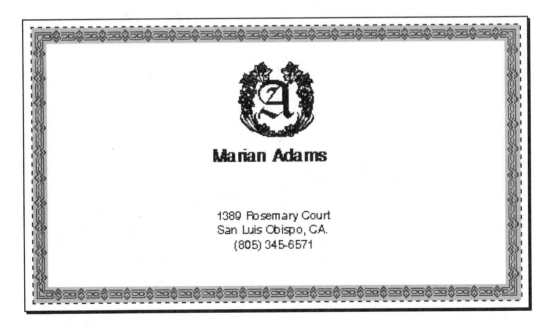

Option 2: Designing a Decorative Number for Use in Projects.

1. Windows: Open the Smart Graphics project from the main menu.
    Macintosh: Open *The Print Shop Companion* and select Smart Graphics.

2. On the next screen is Number Maker. From this screen you select a font,
    style, shape, shadow, position, and color. You also enter the number you
    want in the box to the right of the word number. The Suffix box allows you
    to choose to have the number only or, if it is checked, to have the suffix (st,
    nd, or th) shown also. Three digits are the most you can use.

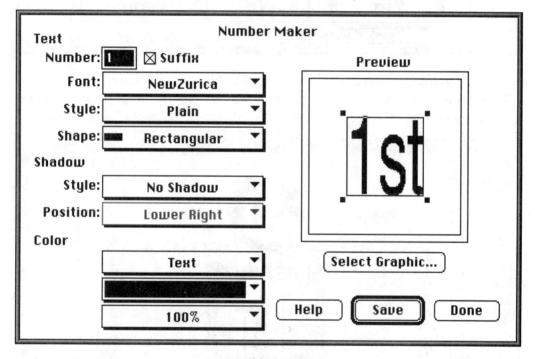

3. To select a Graphic to surround the number, click Select Graphic. From
    this screen you can select specifically designed graphics for the number.
    Click OK and then click Done to return to a screen where the graphic can
    be saved.

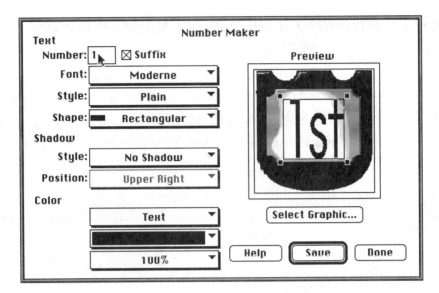

4. A dialog box appears that asks if you want to save the graphic. If you click yes, you are taken to a screen where the items saved in the User Squares folder are listed. Type in a name for your graphic and click Save.

5. Your graphic is saved and ready to use wherever a Square Graphic is needed.

Option 3: Designing a Timepiece to Use in Projects

This option allows you to deign a timepiece graphic to use in your projects.

1. After selecting Timepieces you are presented with the Timepieces screen where you can select the graphic and time. Enter the time you want by highlighting the time boxes and entering the time.

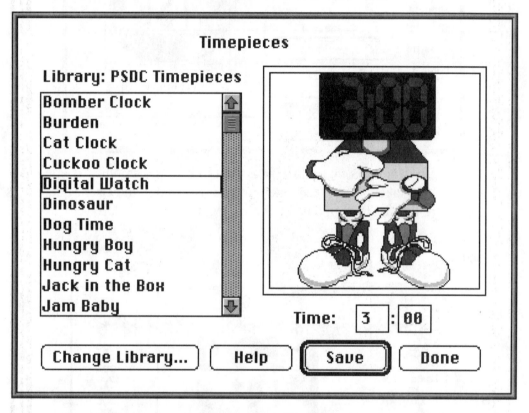

2. To select a Graphic, click on one of the graphics listed. Click Done and return to a screen where the graphic can be saved.

3. A dialog box appears that asks if you want to save the graphic. If you click yes, you are taken to a screen where the items saved in the User Squares folder are listed. Type in a name for your graphic and then Save.

4. Your graphic is now placed in the User Graphic folder on the hard drive to use whenever you have a Square Graphic placeholder.

THE PRINT SHOP PRESSWRITER
WALK THROUGH INDEX

INTRODUCTION TO THE PRINT SHOP PRESSWRITER

The Print Shop PressWriter has six main projects that can be created using the program. The projects are Newsletters, Brochures, Letters and Resumés, Reports, Flyers, and Booklets.

As you explore the various projects, you will find many interesting classroom uses for them.

Students can also benefit from the capabilities of *The Print Shop PressWriter*. Although the following walkthroughs were designed for teacher use, students too can benefit from the content. Duplicate the pages containing the walkthroughs and let your more capable students use them to learn how to use *The Print Shop PressWriter*.

USING THE NEWSLETTER PROJECT

Customize a QuickStart

This category lets you create newsletters for a subject or occassion. Students too can use this project to create newsletters for social studies projects, school special-interest groups, or a myriad of other activities and events. For this walkthrough we are going to make a school newsletter that can be distributed to the school community.

1. Open the Newsletters category from the Project Picker.

2. You now choose from the Customize a QuickStart layout or Start from Scratch Layout. For this project we chose the Customize a QuickStart Layout. From the next screen choose the Classroom model. Click on the model and click OK.

3. The first page of the document appears, ready for your personal touch.

4. To modify the masthead, double-click on the masthead and then drag the mouse over the word Classroom. Key in what you want the newsletter to be titled. In this project we keyed in Classroom News.

5. To personalize the text, start by double-clicking on the headline over the first column of text. Drag the mouse over the headline and key in your own headline.

6. To write text for the column, double-click on the text, highlight it, and enter your own text. If you need a larger view of your document, select View and choose Page Width or even 100% for a really large view.

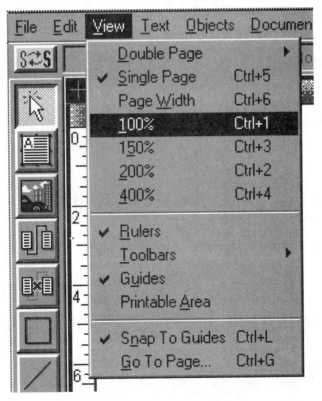

7. To change the font and font size, highlight the text, select Text, and choose Font and Size.

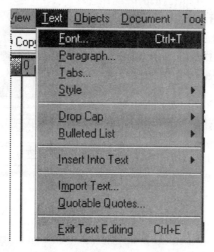

8. To replace the graphic with one of your own choice, double-click on the graphic to be taken immediately to the Graphics Browser screen. From this screen you choose the appropriate graphic for your newsletter.

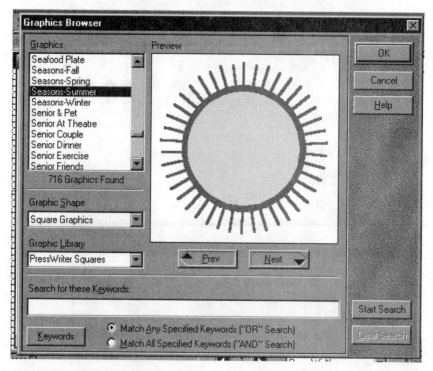

9. To change the Style Set of your newsletter, click on the Style Set button in the upper left corner of the Design Desk.

10. You are now given a choice of Style Sets for a newsletter. Select the one that you prefer and click OK.

11. Continue on with writing your newsletter.

12. To save your newsletter, select File and choose Save.

13. Print the newsletter by selecting File and then Print.

New World News

My Journey

We left Palos hoping to discover a shorter route to the Indies. We really wanted to find those wonderful spices. 33 days after leaving the Canary Islands, we finally set foot on land. I named it San Salvador.

The Ships

We started with three ships. The Nina the Pinto and the Santa Maria. The Santa Maria was wrecked and 40 crew members were left in the West Indies. I wonder how many ships we will be able to sail back when we are ready to return home.

The People

When we landed, we met some people. We did not know their language and we could not talk to them. I tried talking Spanish, Italian, and Portuguese were. They did not answer. We had to use our hands to talk and we had to show them what we wanted.

See you soon, we hope,
C. Columbus

Start from Scratch

1. Select the Start from Scratch layout. For this walkthrough, we wrote a newsletter as if it were written by Columbus and sent to Queen Isabella and her court.

2. The document setup dialog box appears, showing the layouts possible.

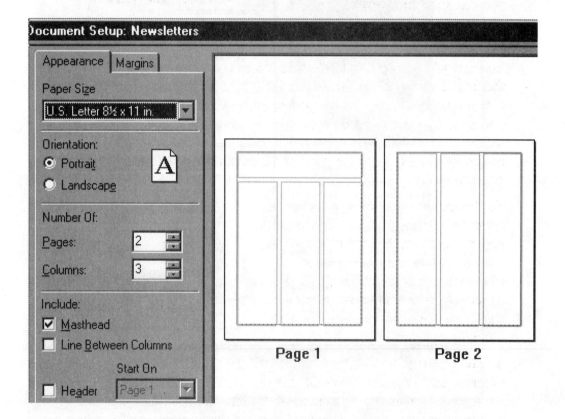

3. For this walkthrough, change the number of columns to 2 by clicking on the arrow in the Columns box to the left of the screen.

4. To write your masthead click on the Selection Tool arrow, and your cursor changes to an arrow. Double-click on the masthead section and write in your title. If you want a different font for the Masthead, highlight the writing and select a font from the Font Menu at the top.

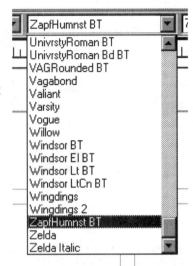

5. To write the text for the columns, click in the first text column and type in your paragraph heading. There you can get a full view of your document by selecting View and then choosing Page Width.

6. You can add a Drop Cap to the first letter of your paragraph. This makes the first letter of the first word much bigger than the rest of the type in the paragraph. Click once on the paragraph, select Text from the menu bar, choose Drop Cap, and then move the mouse to Drop 2 lines. This makes the first letter of the paragraph two lines high and gives a really professional look to the newsletter. You can do this with each of the paragraphs that you write.

7. To change the style set of a document, select the yellow Style Set button in the upper left-hand corner. Click once and you are shown many different styles from which you can choose. Move your mouse arrow down the list; when you click, you see your newsletter in a different style set.

8. To add a graphic to your newsletter, click on the Object icon on the left side of the screen. You can also select Object from the menu bar at the top of the screen. You are given a choice of Square Graphic, Row Graphic, Column Graphic, or Any Graphic Shape. Select the Square Graphic.

To view a full array of graphics, hold your mouse arrow down on the arrow next to the Graphic Library selection.

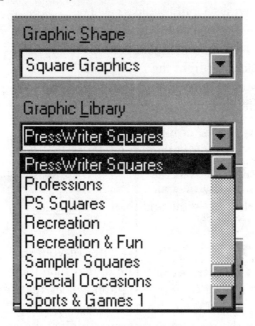

This then gives you a view of all the library choices that you have. After you select a library, a list of all the graphics in that library appears in the upper left-hand corner of the screen. Select one of these graphics by clicking on it or use the Next button under the preview screen.

When you do this, the graphic appears on the page where you are working. Move the graphic to the desired location by putting the mouse arrow in the middle of it and move to the location.

You can also resize the graphic by using the handles surrounding the picture to make it larger or smaller. When you place the graphic on the text, it automatically has text wraparound.

9. To go to the next page, click on the right arrow on the bottom line of the screen.

10. To save the document, Select File and choose Save.

11. To print the document, select Print from the File menu.

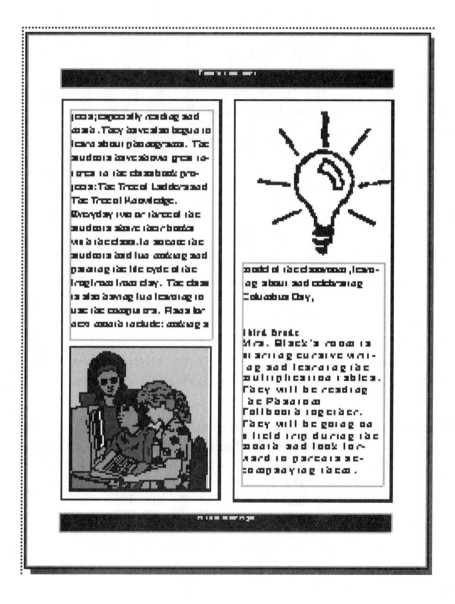

USING THE FLYERS PROJECT

This category has customized layouts that fit almost any type of flyer that you need to produce. The Start from Scratch Layout basically gives you a clear layout on which to place your text and graphics. This project lends itself to all of the various quick flyers you need to announce upcoming events or any of the many classroom announcements sent to the school community. For this walkthrough we are going to make a flyer advertising a fund raising event.

1. Open the Flyers category from the Project Picker and choose whether you want Customized a QuickStart Layout or Start from Scratch. This walkthrough uses the Customize a QuickStart Layout.

2. On the screen you can find 12 different choices of layout. Click on the one you like, and you are taken to a screen where you can modify the layout with your own text and graphics.

3. Double-click in the Masthead area and press delete. Key your headline into the Masthead. You can change the font, style, and size by highlighting the words and choosing the changes from the Text menu at the top of the screen in the Menu bar.

4. To change the graphic, double-click in the graphic area to see handles around the picture. Press delete. Select a graphic from the Object menu. To add a graphic to your flyer, click on the Object icon on the left side of the screen. You can also select Object from the Menu bar at the top of the screen. You are given a choice of Square Graphic, Row Graphic, Column Graphic, or Any Graphic Shape. Select the Square Graphic.

To view a full array of graphics, hold your mouse arrow down on the arrow next to the Graphic Library selection.

5.   Continue modifying the flyer in sections by clicking, deleting, and reentering text. Remember, whenever you want to delete an object, you must highlight it by double-clicking and then press delete.

6.   Save and print your flyer.

Cookies for Computers

Buy cookies at recess to help raise money to buy new software for our school.

3 cookies

25 cents

Location of Event-Playground
January 15, 1999 10:00am
Recess

USING THE REPORTS PROJECT

Start from Scratch

The Report project provides an easy way to create both illustrated covers and written reports. This project is useful for both teachers and students. For this walkthrough we are going to write a report on Totem Poles of the Northeast.

1. Open Report from the Project Picker and select Start from Scratch.

2. The next screen presents the Document Setup: Reports. There are a page one and page two. Click on OK and you are taken to a screen with a blank page on which you can create your report.

3. Start your cover by placing a text box on the page. There are two different ways to enter text:

   • Select the Text box drawing tool icon from the Tool Palette and then draw a text box on the screen.

   • Select Text from the Objects menu from the menu bar.

4. Draw the text box on your screen. Double-click on the inside of the box to get the writing cursor. Now select a font, size, color, and style from the Text menu. This can all be changed after you enter the text. Remember, to change text, you need to highlight the text first and then make the appropriate changes.

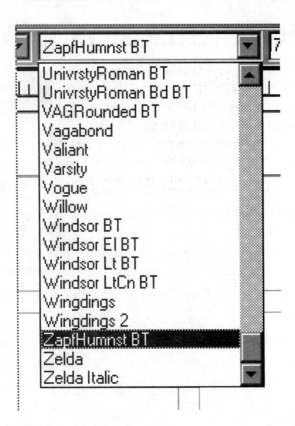

5. Key in your text.

6. There are several ways to add a graphic to your report page.

- Select Square Graphic from the Object menu and choose one of the square graphics from the libraries.

- You are then presented with the folders that are available.

- Double-click on a folder to have the pictures listed. To choose a graphic, double-click on the folder and then select a graphic from it. When you select a graphic, click once to have the graphic shown in the preview window. It is in this window that you can crop the image and customize it to meet your graphic needs.

- Move your cursor over the picture and drag a box over the part of the picture that you want.

- Click open to import the image. The image is then shown on your screen. You can now move and resize the picture.

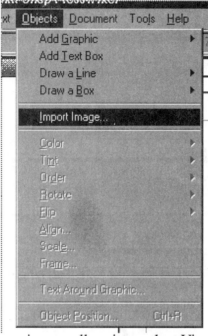

7. To see the whole page in a smaller view, select View from the menu bar and choose Single Page. You can also choose to view the page even larger by choosing 100% from the View menu.

8. Use the page turner at the bottom of the screen to go to page two. Use the Text Box drawing tool to make a text box on the page. After drawing the box, click outside the box and then double-click inside the box to get the insert cursor. Now you can choose a font, size, color, and style for your text. Select Font from the Text menu and make your choices.

9. Add a graphic to the page, and the second page of the report is finished.

10. Save and print your report.

The Figures carved on the totem represent sky, river, forest, sea, and mountain beings from the family. They tell the family legends of how ancestors have taken these beings as their family crest. The poles last up to one hundred years. When the old totem pole falls, it is allowed to rest where it has fallen and a new one is carved. There are four basic types of poles: Frontal, house posts, memorial poles, and mortuary poles.

The totem tells others which clan lives in the house. Wood carving is a big art and today use traditional designs. The crests on the totem are much the same as the European coat of arms.

Customize a QuickStart

For this walkthrough we are going to make a cover for a report.

1. Open Reports from the project picker.

2. The next screen lets you choose to Customize a QuickStart Layout or the Start from Scratch Layout.

3. For this project we chose to use Customize a QuickStart Layout. There are eight choices of Layouts from which to choose. We chose layout F-Report. Click on the layout you want and click OK to place it on the screen.

4. Double-click in the text area that you want to change. In this case we needed to change the Report Name to Our Capital. Highlight the text and key in the title. If you want to change font, size, style, and color, use the Text menu to select the desired elements.

5. If you want to eliminate any text, highlight the text and press delete.

6. There are several ways to add a graphic to your report page.

   • Select Square Graphic from the Object menu and choose one of the Square Graphics from the libraries.

   • To import a graphic from a CD-ROM or the hard drive, you need to tell the computer where the graphic is located. Choose the Import Image from the Objects menu to display the Import Image dialog box.

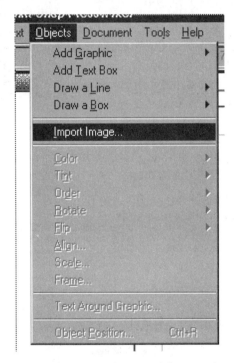

   • Click on the directory where the graphics are located. You are then presented with the folders that are available.

   • Double-click on a folder to have the pictures listed. To choose a graphic, double-click on the folder and then select a graphic from it. When you select a graphic, click once to have the graphic shown in the preview window. It is in this window that you can crop the image and customize it to meet your graphic needs.

   • Move your cursor over the picture and drag a box over the part of the picture that you want.

- Click Open to import the image. The image is then shown on your screen . You can now move and resize the picture

7. To see the whole page in a smaller view, select View from the menu bar and choose Single Page. You can also choose to view the page even larger.

8. We have now designed the cover for the report. To save the cover, select File and choose Save.

9. Now it is time to write the report. At the bottom of the screen are the page turner arrows. Click on the right arrow, and you are taken to page two of the report project. You can click and then highlight text, and enter your own text if you want to use the predesigned layout. If you want a blank page on which to write the report, simply click once to get the handles and press delete. Do that on the various sections of the page, and you will then have a blank page.

10. There are two different ways to enter text:

   - Select the Text box drawing tool icon from the tool palette and then draw a text box on the screen.

   - Select text from the Objects menu from the menu bar.

11. Draw the text box on your screen. Double-click on the inside of the box to get the writing cursor. Now select a font, size, color and style from the Text menu. This can all be changed after you enter the text.

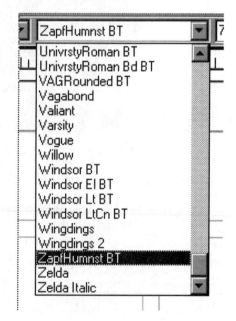

12. Type in your text.

13. Save and print.

USING THE LETTERS AND RESUMÉS PROJECT

Customize a Layout

This category provides many quick avenues to writing stylish letters and resumés. For this walkthrough you are going to write a letter on distinctive letterhead paper.

1. Open Letters and Resumés from the Project Picker.

2. For this walkthrough, choose CQSLayout

3. There are 13 choices of layouts.

4. For this project choose H-Layout.

5. Click on the layout, and the next screen shows the layout ready for your modifications.

6. Double-click on the heading and highlight and delete it. Enter your own text.

7. For the text of the letter; highlight and delete the text and then enter your own.

8. You can change your font, size, style, and color by selecting Text from the menu bar and then Font.

Start from Scratch

Try having students write resumés as if they were a famous person applying for a job. For this walk-through we are going to make a resumé for an English Royal Guard applying for a new job.

1. Open Letters or Resumés from the project picker. Select Letters and Resumé and choose the Start from Scratch layout.

2. To place a row graphic across the top or bottom of the page, select the Graphics icon and choose a row graphic. You might need to search through the various graphics libraries to find just the right graphic.

3. Use the Add Text box from the Object menu to create an area for your text. You can change font, size, and style by highlighting your text and then making the changes.

4. Add a Square Graphic to your resumé, if needed, by choosing Square Graphic from the Object menu.

5. Save and print your resumé.

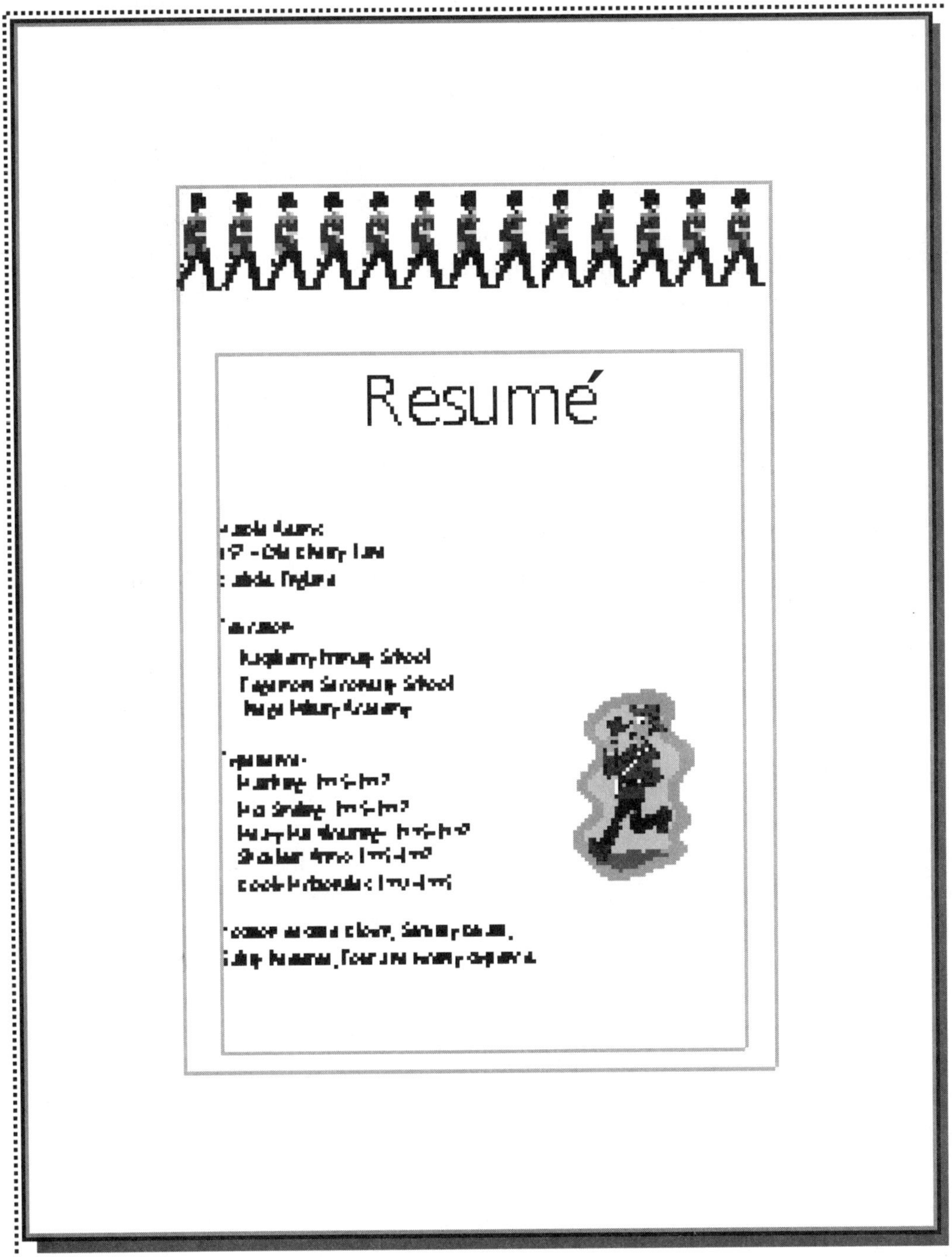

Resumé

(illegible text)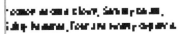

USING THE BROCHURES PROJECT

Customize a QuickStart Layout

The Brochures project lets you and your students create really creative hard copy for augmentation of projects such as social studies reports, forming special-interest clubs, and informing the school community of important events and occasions. For this walkthrough we are going to make a brochure for the Computer Club at our school.

1. Open Brochures from the Project Picker.

2. You can now select Customize or Start from Scratch from the next screen. For this project we chose Customize and then the A-Brochure. Use the scroll bar to move down to see all 20 possible layouts.

3. You are now taken to a screen where you can customize your layout.

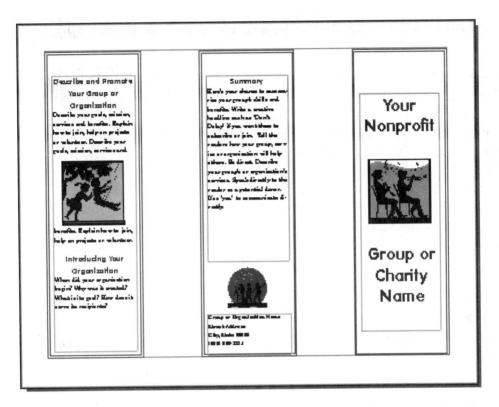

4. To enlarge the brochure to make it easier to write and design, use the View menu to change to 100% or more.

5. Highlight and then delete the text at the top of the graphic so that you can insert your own text.

6. To add a graphic, click on the graphic presently on the page and press delete. You may add the graphic first and then highlight the old graphic and press delete. Select Object from the tool bar menu or from the menu bar at the top of the screen and choose Square Graphic. You are then taken immediately to the Graphics Browser screen. From this screen you can choose the appropriate graphic for your brochure.

7. To add a line going across the page, select Object from the menu and choose the draw a line tool. From the pop-up menu, select the line tool that you want. Move the cross-hair cursor over the page, and line appears.

8. Save and print.

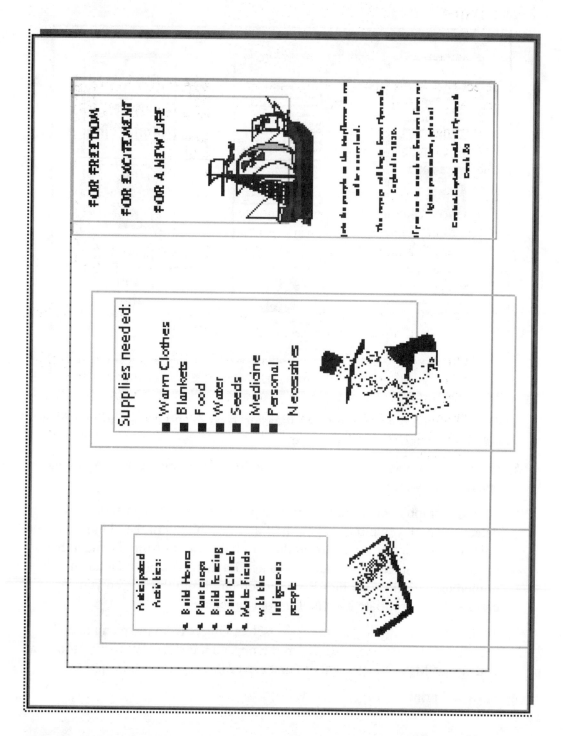

Start from Scratch

Using the Start from Scratch layout lets you have more choices as to text and graphic placement.

1. Select Brochures from the project picker and select Start from Scratch.

2. This brings you to the Document Setup for Brochures menu where you can choose a setup.

3. On the next screen you can choose the number of columns. You can also choose to put a line between the columns. To see your work in a larger format, select View and choose the size that you wish to use for working.

4. For this project we are making a brochure advertising for people to join the voyage on the Mayflower to settle in the New World.

5. From the Object menu, select Add a Text box. You now have a text box. Enter the text and modify the font, size, and style by highlighting the text and selecting Text from the menu. To use bullets in your text, select Text and choose Bulleted List. Choose which type of bullet you want. The bullets will appear in front of each sentence until you rechoose Text and choose none.

6. To add a graphic, select the Object menu and choose to Add a Graphic Square.

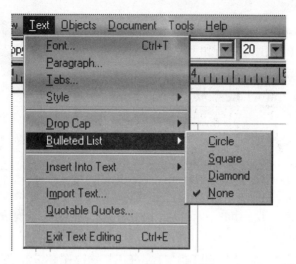

7. View your document and look for areas that you might want to change.

8. Save and print.

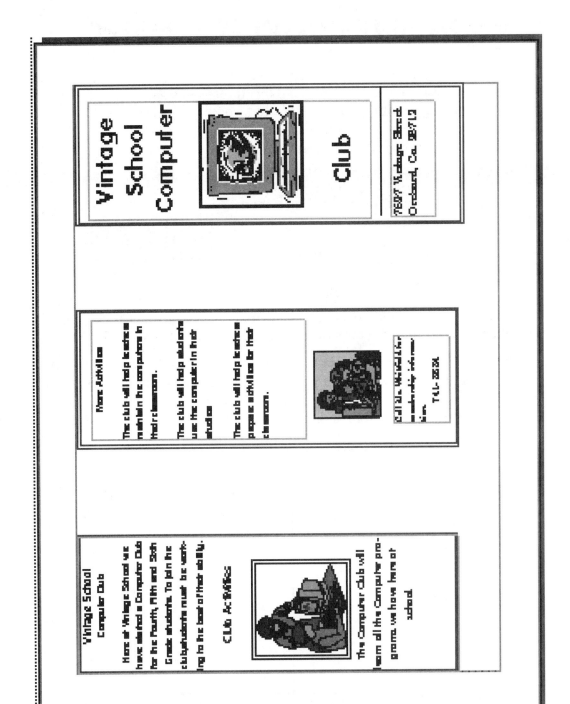

USING THE BOOKLETS PROJECT

This project lets you make a variety of materials in booklet format. Key children's stories into this format and print an original children's book. Reword favorite classroom books to meet the reading needs of various students. Write short books with social science information. Write math stories to print in booklet format. The printout is on two pages with two sections each. In this walkthrough we are making a short reading book for younger readers.

1. Open the Booklets project from the project picker.

2. You can now choose either a QuickStart Layout or a Start from Scratch layout. For this walkthrough, the Start from Scratch layout was chosen. Click on Start from Scratch and click OK.

3. The next screen shows the layout for the front and the back of the booklet. On the right side of the screen you design the cover. On the left portion of the screen, you design the last page or back of the book. To design your booklet using a larger format on the screen, choose 100% from the View menu on the menu bar.

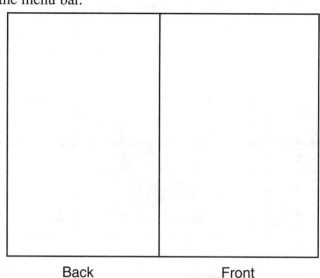

Back   Front

4. To write the title of the booklet, select the Add Text box from the Object menu on the menu bar. Draw a text box in the area where you want the title. You'll notice handles around the text box. Now double-click in the text box and a cursor appears. Key in your title. If the title is too small, highlight the text and select a different size from the size menu at the top of the screen.

5. To place a graphic, select Add Graphic and then Square Graphic from the Object menu in the menu bar. Double-click on the Square Graphic and choose the one you want from the graphics selection presented or choose Change Libraries and select the graphic.

6. To add any other text to the front, select the Add Text box and follow the directions in number 5.

7. Now compose the text and choose graphics for the back of the booklet.

8. To write the story on the two inside pages, click on the arrow at the bottom of the screen and go to page two. On this page write your text and add the graphics.

9. When you are finished, save and print the booklet. Assemble, fold, and staple together. You can also print the four sides on one piece of paper by printing the front and back pages on one side and then turning it over, reinserting it, and printing the inside two pages on the other side.

Felix kissed his Mother good-night.
Felix kissed his Father good-night.
Felix licked his whiskers, closed his eyes and went to sleep.

He dreamed the favorite dream of all cats. He dreamed of his birthday party.

The hands on the clock said 7:00. It was bedtime for Felix the cat.
Mother said, "It is time for bed."
Father said, "It is time for bed."
Felix said, "It is time for milk and cookies."
"All right," said Mother.
"All right," said Father.
"Yum, Yum," said Felix.

THE PRINT SHOP TEACHER PROJECTS INDEX

MAKING CLASSROOM BANNERS

Decorating the classroom with banners makes the room colorful and calls attention to special events and activities. Banners can be used in other ways also. Students can make banners announcing their reports. For this project you will be making a banner advertising "Back to School Night."

1. Open Banners from the project menu. Select the orientation that you want.

2. The next screen presents choices for Backdrops. For this project choose Blank Page and click OK.

3. The next screen allows for a choice of layouts. Scroll through and see the various layouts possible. For this banner choose Banner 1 and click OK.

4. You see a large display of your banner layout along with the number of pages that will be used.

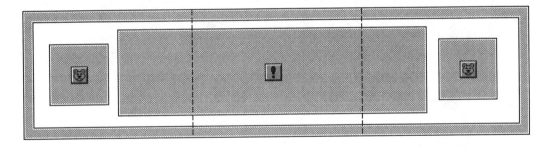

5. Double-click on the Headline placeholder and you are taken to the Banner Text dialog screen. Key in the text that you want. You can change font, shape, size, and justification from this screen. If you want to change color, click on Customize and select a color from the palette.

6. To add Square Graphics to the banner, double-click on the Square Graphic placeholder, and you are taken to the Square Graphic selection menu. You might need to change libraries. The graphic used in this sample project is from the Graphics Collection CD-ROM in the Learning folder. When you select the graphic, click in the Apply to all Squares box and the graphic will be in both of the squares.

7. To change the direction of the graphic, select the graphic by clicking in it once to get the handles. Now, select the Flip Tool in the tool palette, hold down the mouse button, and select horizontal. You have now flipped the graphic.

8. To add a border to the frame, double-click on the border that is greyed out and select an appropriate border. Click OK.

9. To customize a banner so that you can add more graphics than just the original placeholders, you need to add Square Graphics. Select Objects from the menu bar, then select Add, and finally select Square Graphics. When the graphic is placed, resize it by moving the handles diagonally. Move it to where you want it placed and double-click to access the graphics dialog box. Continue in this manner to add more graphics to the banner.

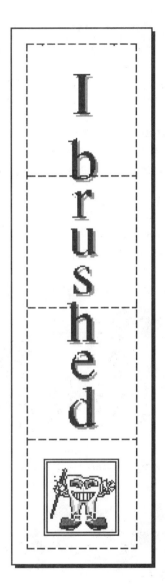

MAKING TENT MARKERS

Labeling learning centers and classroom displays with tent markers makes the centers and displays clearly definable and graphically attractive. Using the Greeting Card project lets you spend only a few minutes creating the tents that enhance your classroom environment. In this particular project you will be making a tent marker for the classroom science center and seeing examples of classroom library, science center, and student of the day tent markers.

Making a Science Tent Marker

1. Select the Greeting Card project from the main menu.

2. On the next screen, select the Top Fold greeting card style.

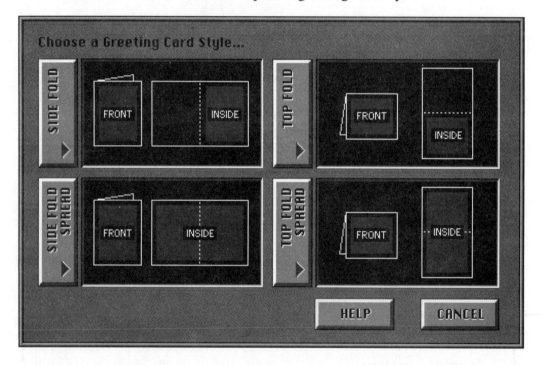

3. The next screen offers choices for the Landscape Backdrops. For this project choose Blank Page by double-clicking on it or click once and press OK.

4. At the next screen you choose your Landscape Layout. The layouts are predesigned and you only have to choose the one that has the elements that you need. For example, Number 25 just has a text box while Number 23 has text, headline, column graphics, and a placeholder for line graphics. For your first tent choose Greeting Card 16. Click OK.

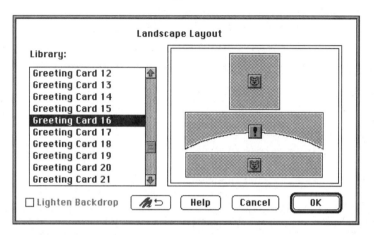

5. On your screen is a large display of the layout. There are placeholders for Square Graphic, Headline, and Row Graphics. Double-click on the Square Graphic. This takes you to a screen where you can choose the appropriate graphic for your tent marker. If there are no graphics listed on the screen that you want, then you need to change libraries and select from them. To change libraries, click on the Change Library button and select the place where the libraries are located.

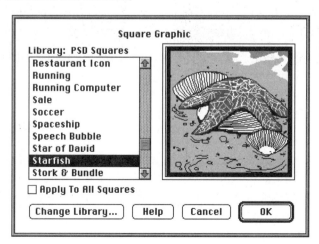

6. Now double-click on the headline placeholder, and you are taken to the Headline Text screen where you can choose font and shape and customize your text. To change the font, select from the Font menu by holding down the arrow and moving your mouse to the desired font. Type in your text for the science tent marker.

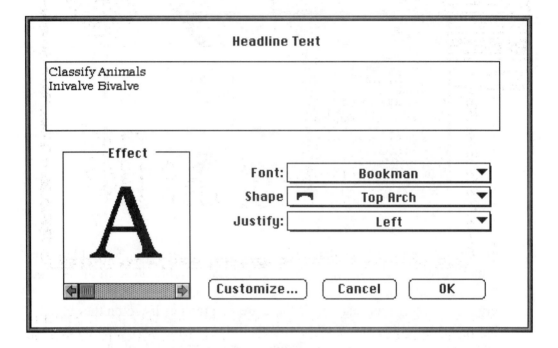

7. Next double-click on the Row Graphic placeholder and select an appropriate graphic. Remember that if you need more graphic choices, click on the Change Library button and make your selection.

8. To add a border, you can choose border from the Object icon in the tool menu bar or you can select Object from the menu bar, drag to Add, and move your mouse down to Border. Double-click on the greyed border area, select a border from the choices, and click OK.

9. You can change the color of the graphic that you chose very easily. Click on the graphic once to highlight it, and you will get handles around the graphic. When the handles appear around the graphic, it means that the computer can work with it. To change color, select the Color line in the Tool Bar and move to the color of your choice.

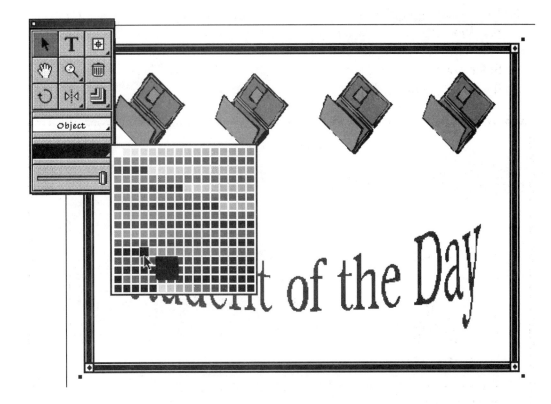

You can change the border colors the same way. Just click on the border to get the handles and change color by using the color selection in the tool bar. Note: Only solid borders can change color. Borders made up of patterns will not.

10. To print the tent marker, select Print from the File menu. If you want heavier paper for the marker, print on card stock. Yes, it will go through your printer. The front of the greeting card will be the tent marker and the remaining parts will be blank.

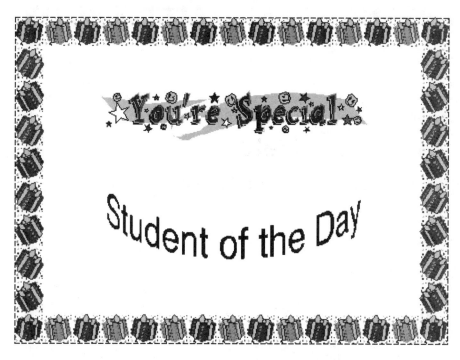

MAKING BIG AND LITTLE BOOKS

Big and little books are so easy to make using the Sign project. Have students dictate books to you and print them using the various printing options available. Use favorite fairy tales and excerpts from classroom read novels and have students help choose the graphics and layouts. In this project a favorite story was used to produce a big book and accompanying regular sized books. Imagine having the big book in the library along with copies of the book in smaller sizes.

Making Big Books Using Pre-Drawn Backgrounds

1. From the main menu, select Sign.

2. Select the Tall option from the next screen.

3. From the proposed backgrounds, choose a background that compliments your story.

4. To write the story, select the Text option from the Tool Palette.

5. Hold the mouse button down and drag diagonally to create a box in which you will write the text.

6. If the text is too large for the text box, highlight the text and choose Text from the menu bar. Select Size from the Text menu and choose a smaller size.

7. Save the first page of your big book by selecting Save from the File menu. Choose a name for the page and put the number one so that you will know which page it is when you want to print.

8. Repeat the directions for subsequent pages.

9. To print in the big book size, select Print from the File menu. Select More Options from the Print menu.

10. On the next screen, choose 4x4 from the Project Size option, and your page or pages will print out poster size. Tape the pieces together, and you have a page for a big book. Continue with the other pages.

Jack and the Beanstalk

Jack and the Beanstalk

There was once upon a time a poor widow who had an only son named Jack and a cow named Milky-White. All they had to live on was the milk the cow gave, which they carried to the market and sold.

Jack took the cow to market to sell it. He hadn't gone far when he met a funny-looking old man who said, "Good morning and where are you off to?" I'll trade your cow for these beans. If you plant them overnight, by morning they will grow right up to the sky." He handed the man Milky-White and took the beans home to his mother.

The next morning when Jack woke up, the room looked funny. The sun was shining into part of it, but the rest was dark and shady. The beans had sprung up into a big beanstalk which went up and up and up like a ladder until it reached the sky. Jack jumped onto the beanstalk and up he climbed until he reached the clouds and found a great tall house.

Making Big Books using Your Own Layout

1. Choose Sign from the project menu.

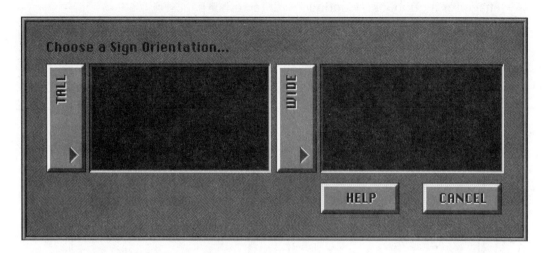

2. Select the Blank Page option and on the next screen choose a layout that presents your text and graphics well. Refer to the section in this book on Using the Sign Project on page 20. You might choose to have no layout and then create your own using the Object menu choices.

3. To make a book with a coloring book format where students can cooperatively color the pictures, choose Coloring Book from the selections in the More Options menu found on the Print dialog screen.

MAKING SPECIALIZED CALENDARS/LOGS

Using the calendar project from *The Print Shop* you make a weekly log form for students to record their television viewing habits. After the log is completed you create graphics showing the amount of time spent in school as opposed to the amount of time viewing TV. Using this graph, you can guide students into finding other forms of recreation.

1. Select the Calendar project, and then choose Weekly from the Calendar Type dialog box on the next screen.

2. Select Tall from the Calendar Orientation menu.

3. From the next screen, select the Month, Year, and Starting Day. Click OK when your selections have been made.

4. From the Portrait Backdrop choose the Blank Page option. Click OK.

5. From the Portrait Layout screen select Calendar 1. You have a Headline placeholder as well as a Square Graphic placeholder.

6. Double-click in the Headline Placeholder and the date and year appear. If it is not the date that you want in the Headline, double-click on the Headline text to be taken to the Headline Text dialog box. Here you can delete the current text and choose your font, style, and size.

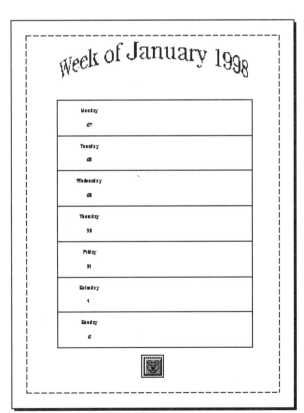

7. To place a graphic on the calendar, double-click on the Square Graphic placeholder. The TV graphic used in this project is located in the Library: Calendar Icons.

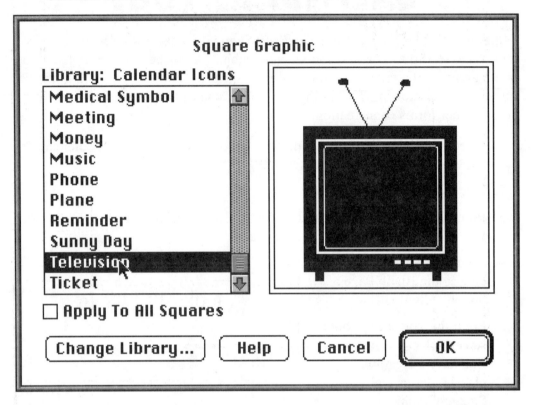

8. To add a title to the weekly log, insert a Text Block. Select Object from the main menu, choose Add, and move to Text Block. When the Text Block appears, hold down the mouse button and move it to where you want it placed. Double-click and write your text.

9. To add a border to the log, select Object from the tool bar and choose border. Double-click in the greyed out border area on the screen and choose your border.

10. Print your weekly log.

Week of January 1998

Monday 27	
Tuesday 28	
Wednesday 29	
Thursday 30	
Friday 31	
Saturday 1	
Sunday 2	

T.V. Viewing

MAKING A CLASSROOM PRESENTATIONS CALENDAR

The schedule for students giving their science reports can be put onto a calendar that is printed in large size and posted on the classroom bulletin board for all to refer to.

1. Select Calendar from the main project screen and then choose Monthly from the next screen. Choose Wide from the Calendar Orientation screen.

2. From the next screen select the year and month for your calendar. Click OK.

3. Select the Blank Page option and then choose a Landscape Layout from the next screen. For this project choose Calendar 3. This provides an area for the headline and an area for a border. You can also add a Square Graphic to the calendar.

4. Double-click on the border area and select a border.

5. To list the students on the calendar day on which they are presenting, double-click on the date on the calendar. You are then taken to an Edit Calendar Day dialog screen. Click on the Edit Text button. That takes you to the Edit Text screen. Type in your text. You can select the 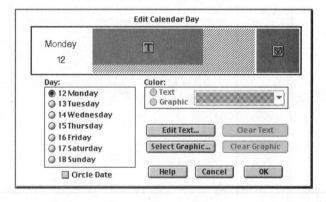 font, style, size, and color before you write. If you want to change the font and size of the text after you have keyed it in, highlight the text and make the changes from this dialog box. Click OK. On the next screen you can still make choices, but if all is fine, click OK again. The text is placed in the date box.

Edit Text

Font:	**Justification:**
NewZurica ▼	Left ▼

30
Howard
Brown

Style:

☒ Plain   ☐ Underline

☐ Bold   ☐ Outline

☐ Italic   ☐ Shadow

Placement:

Top ▼

Color:

▼

Size:

12   Large ▼

(Help)   (Cancel)   (OK)

6. To print the calendar in large size, select Print from the File menu and then choose More Options. Select the size you want.

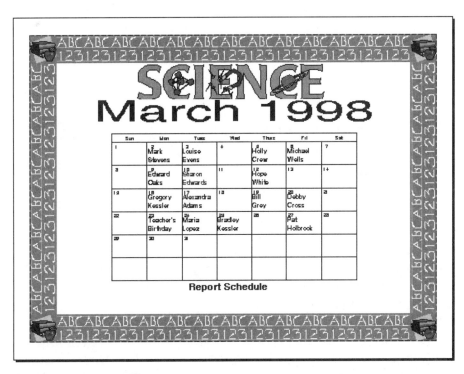

Making a Classroom Schedule

A large calendar on which all the special events for the classroom are listed can be made easily and displayed in a prominent place in the classroom. This helps students keep track of their time.

1. Select the Calendar Project from the project menu and choose Monthly and Tall.

2. Select Blank Page from the next menu and set the month, year, and date.

3. On the Portrait Layout screen, select Calendar 8 for this activity.

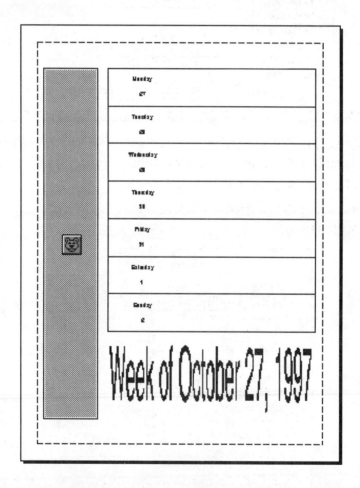

4. Double-click on the Column placeholder and choose a graphic.

5. To write the events of the week, double-click on the day area. You are now taken to the Edit Calendar Day screen.

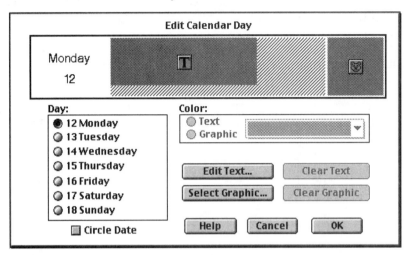

6. Double-click in the Text placeholder area, and you now have a blank area in which to write. Choose a size for the font. You might want to change the font also. Type in your text and click OK.

7. Now to add a graphic, double-click in the Square Graphic placeholder and select a graphic.

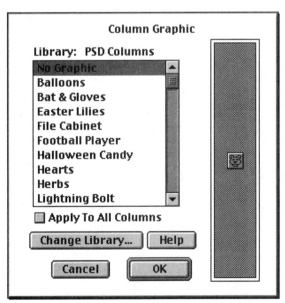

8. Repeat the above procedure until you have listed the dates for your classroom.

9. To add a border to the calendar, select Object, then Add, and then Border. Double-click on the greyed border and choose a border.

10. To make a large print for the bulletin board, select Print from the File menu and choose More Options and the size you want.

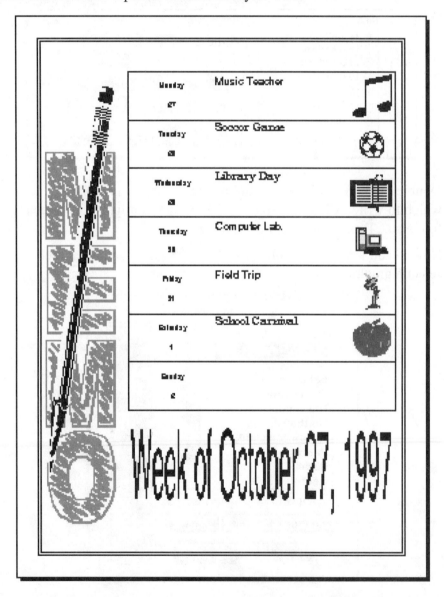

MAKING GAME CARDS AND/OR FLASH CARDS

Using the Business Card project, teachers can create game cards for individualized, teacher-created game boards, as well as various type of business cards for themselves and their students. In this activity you will make a set of game cards. Each card in the set will have the same design so that you can easily keep them together for the individual games. On the back of the cards you can write any questions that you want answered before the players proceed in the game.

Game Cards

1. Select the Business Card project from the main menu of *The Print Shop Companion* if you are using a Macintosh or from the main menu of *The Print Shop* if you are using Windows.

2. Choose the Wide Orientation and then select Blank Page.

3. Choose No Layout from the Layout dialog box. This enables you to create the type of layout that suits your game cards best.

4. From the Object menu choose a Square Graphic and place it on the card. You can also add text by choosing a Text Block from the Object menu.

5. To add a border, select border from the Object menu. Double-click on the greyed area and choose a border.

6. When you have completed your design, print the cards. The cards will print ten to a page.

7. Use the guides to cut the cards apart.

Flash Cards

1. To make a set of flash cards, choose the Tall orientation and then a Layout or choose No Layout.

2. Choose a Backdrop for the cards.

3. For the activity illustrated here, choose No Layout and Letters and Numbers from the Premium Collection.

4. Just select Add Square from the Object menu.

5. To add a border to the card, select border from the Object menu. Double-click on the greyed border and select a border.

6. This orientation prints ten to a page.

MAKING PERSONAL STATIONERY AND CLASSROOM PASSES

By using the Postcard project, teachers can make personalized messages in multiples for easy distribution. Postcards print four to a page and then can be cut apart and put into packets. They also can be taken to a printer or copy center and made into pads. The following directions are for making personalized message pads.

1. Open the Post Card project from the main menu of *The Print Shop Companion* if you are using a Macintosh, or from the main menu of *The Print Shop* if you are using Windows.

2. Choose the Wide Orientation and then Blank Page and click OK.

3. From the Landscape Layout, choose No Layout and click OK.

4. You are presented with a blank postcard front which you can now design.

5. For the Tele-Thought activity illustrated here, you need to use two text boxes for the different sizes of text. First select a Text Block from the Object menu and place it near the top of the post card.

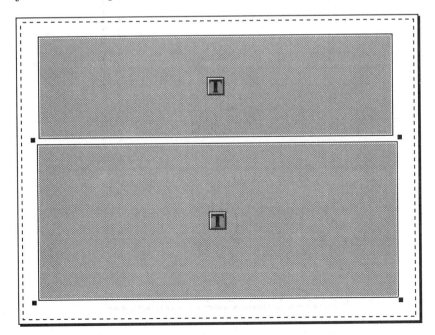

6. Double-click in the top Text Block. Type in the title of the note: "TELE-THOUGHT." Now, double-click on the lower Text Block and write in the rest of the message.

7. To add a graphic, select Square Graphic from the Object menu. Place it in the desired location, size it, and double-click on the Placeholder to choose your graphic.

8. Print your messages. They will print four to a page.

TELE-THOUGHT

To: From:

To express gratitude is to send forth a warm, friendly feeling of thankfulness for kindness received. Every time you have a loving thought about someone, give a Tele-Thought and watch it brighten their day. (and yours!)

   I'm so glad we're friends
   Thank you for _____
   I appreciate you!
   I think you're neat!
   That was just great!

CONFERENCE:

DAY: TIME:

MAKING LARGE POSTERS FOR CLASSROOM USE

Large posters of poems that the class is studying or that are significant to other class studies can be made easily with the Sign project. From nursery rhymes to famous quotes, all can be published for use in the classroom. Original poetry written by students and published in a large format is exciting and motivating. In this particular project we will be making large prints of a famous poem, a nursery rhyme, a song, and a vocabulary chart.

1. Select Sign from the main project menu. From the next screen choose the Tall option.

2. Choose Blank Page as the Landscape Backdrop and click OK and choose No Layout for the layout. Click OK. This gives you a blank surface on which to create.

3. To choose a graphic for the poster, select the Object icon from the Tool Palette and choose Square Graphic. The icon for the Square Graphic appears on your screen. Double-click to choose the graphic. If you do not find a graphic in the group that is shown on the screen, click on the Change Library button and tell the computer where the other graphics are located. (You might have to locate *The Print Shop* on your hard drive and then locate the libraries.) Click on the graphic, and it is placed on your screen. You can then move the graphic to where you would prefer it to be by putting your mouse arrow in the middle of the graphic, holding down the mouse button, and moving it.

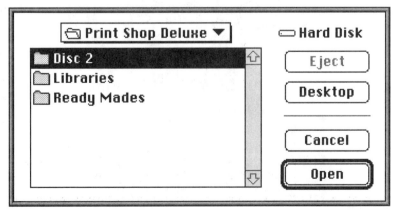

4. To place text on your poster, select the Text icon from the Tool Palette and drag to the size of the text box you want. Type in your text. You can make font, size, and style changes by highlighting the text and selecting Text from the menu bar and choosing Font, Style, or Size options.

5. To change the color of the text, highlight the text. On the Tool Palette, notice that the word text appears in the bottom half and the color of the text shows below. This means that you can change the color of the text by holding down the arrow next to the color and selecting a color.

6. You can also insert a text box by selecting Object from the menu bar and choosing Insert Text Block. The Text Block appears on the screen, and you just move it to where you want it placed. You can also enlarge it by moving the handles. Double-click on the Text Block and write your text.

7. Follow the directions in Number 4 but choose Row Graphic instead of Square Graphic and place a row graphic.

8. To add a border to your poster, select Object from the menu bar or select the Object icon from the Tool Palette and choose Border. A greyed border appears around your poster.

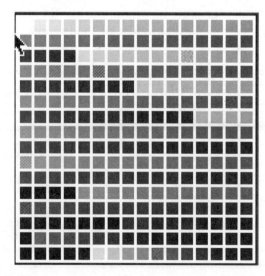

9. Double-click inside the greyed border, and you are presented with border choices. Select a border, and it is placed on your poster. You can Change Libraries for borders as you do in the Square Graphics choices.

10. To print in standard size, just select Print from the File menu.

11. If you want to print in a larger mode, select Print from the File menu and then select More Options in the lower left-hand corner. The next menu lets you choose the size of your poster. You can choose from one page to four pages wide and four pages long. You can also print in Coloring Book mode and have your students color the graphics.

Old Mrs. Witch, old Mrs. Witch, tell me what you see, tell me what you see.
I see a little Jack o' Lantern looking at me.

Other Ideas:

- Use a transparency in your printer instead of paper to make an overhead to use for classroom presentations.

- Large sized books or big books

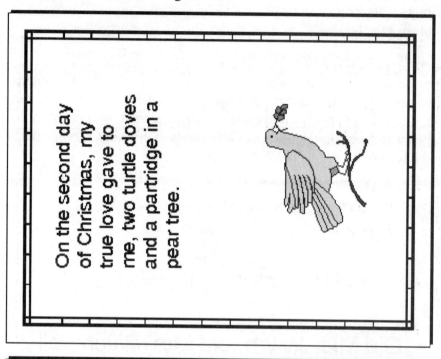

- If you need to make a presentation to a peer group, use the transparency in your printer and then display it on an overhead.

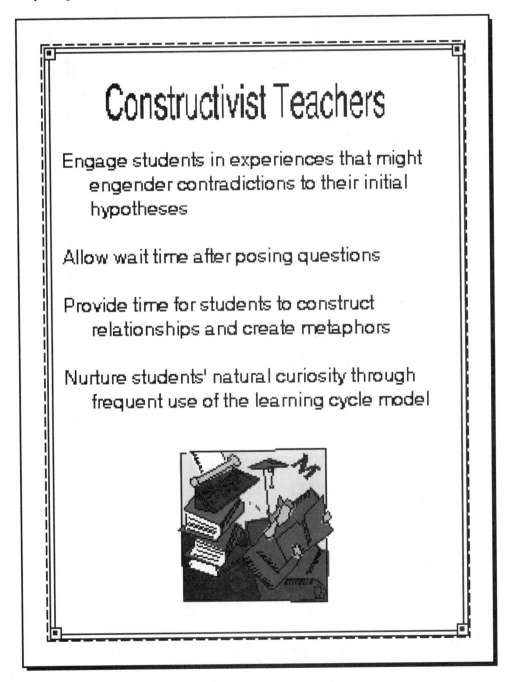

- Create vocabulary posters for English/Spanish or for other language books.

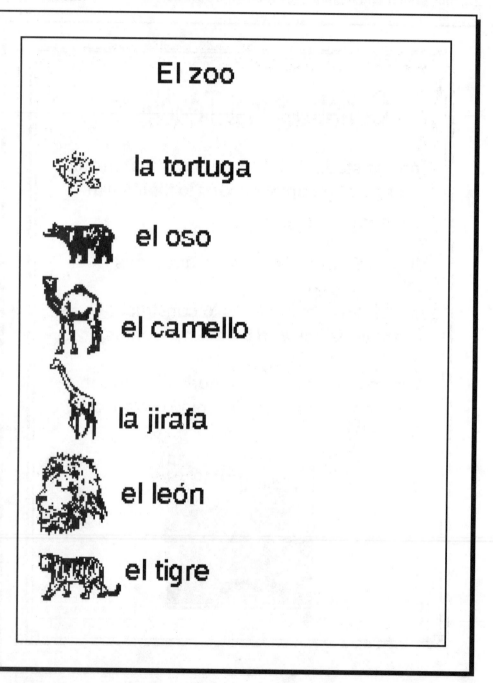

- Perpare large poster for the classroom and a smaller one for individual use.

MAKING EDUCATOR BUSINESS CARDS

Educators are always being asked for their business cards, by parents, vendors at trade shows, attendees at conferences or people at community meetings. The following activity takes you through making a very attractive business card. It is easily modified so that if you save the card, you can make changes as you change classrooms or assignments.

1. Select Business Cards from the main project menu.

2. Select the Orientation you desire and from the next screen choose a Landscape Backdrop. If you want a backdrop for this particular activity, choose School 4. Click OK. Then choose Layout 4 and click OK.

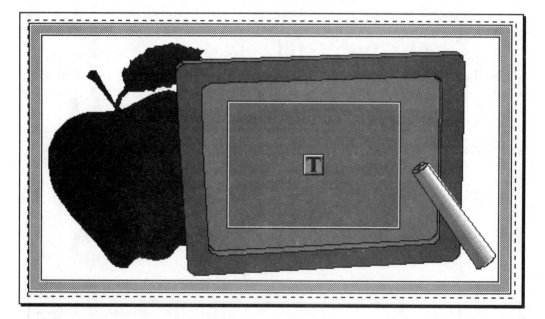

3. Double-click on the Text placeholder and type in your text.

4. You can change text size, style, and font by highlighting and using the choices in the Text menu.

- If you want to design your card from scratch, select Blank Page and then No Layout. Now just add the Text Block, Square Graphic, and Border and then print. This prints ten to a page.

MAKING LETTERHEADS

Letterhead stationery is an essential part of a teacher's supplies. Not only are teachers sending notes home to students and families but also to other personnel and, of course, the office. After you design a letterhead for yourself, you might want to take it to a copy shop to make a large supply of copies quickly and inexpensively. You might even have them make your design into a notepad by applying glue.

Making a Notepad Using a Layout

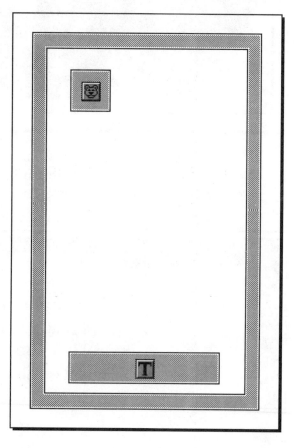

1. Select Letterhead from the projects menu. From the Letterhead Size menu select Notepad. You can select a Backdrop from the Notepad Backdrop dialog box or select Blank Page. For this particular activity, choose Blank Page and click OK.

2. The next screen allows you to choose your layout or to choose No Layout. For this activity choose Notepad1.

3. Double-click on the text placeholder. Type in your text.

4. Double-click on the Square Graphic and choose an appropriate graphic.

5. Double-click on the greyed-out border and choose a border for the notepad.

6. When your notepad is finished, select File and choose Print.

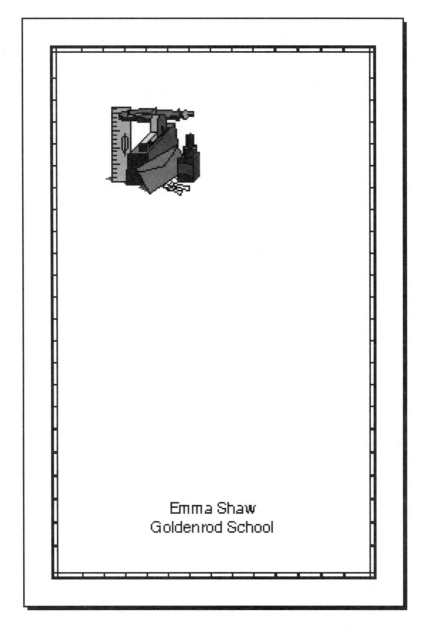

Note: Be sure to save this on a disk for use after supplies run out.

Making Stationery with Large Writing Areas

1. If you choose a layout with a large text area, you can design the page with graphics and text. Leave the large text box untouched, and it prints out blank.

Layout with Text on Top of Graphics

1. You can place text on top of graphics for a really sharp looking letterhead. Select the layout that you want and double-click on the Headline placeholder. Type in your text.

2. To place a graphic, select the Objects icon from the tool menu or select Object from the menu bar and place the Square Graphic on the screen. Double-click on the placeholder and select a graphic.

3. To place the graphic behind the text, move it to the text area and with the graphic highlighted, select Object and choose Order. Make the choice to put the graphic behind or in front of the text.

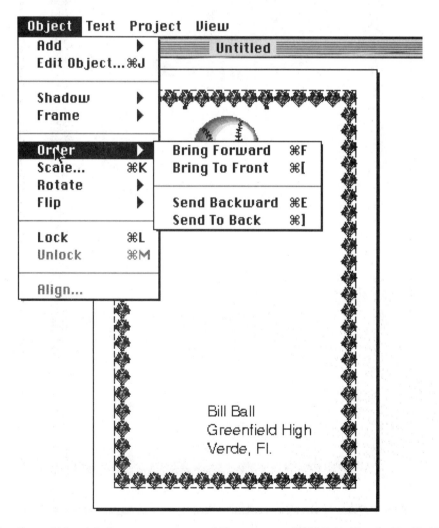

More Ideas:

- Print paper to be used in a writing center. Students write their drafts and, if a computer and printer are available, they use the paper to write letters as if they are the persons to whom the notepaper belongs.

- Carmen SanDiego could be writing of her adventures eluding the detectives.

MAKING CERTIFICATES

Personalized certificates can be used as rewards for many different types of achievements. Thanking parent volunteers, recognizing student improvement in sports, academics, and behavior can all be done with certificates. Another creative use for certificates is to use the historical signatures provided with the program to give a historical context to a past event.

There are a myriad of Ready Mades Certificates available for your use. These can be accessed by selecting Ready Mades from the Certificate orientation screen. This screen is presented after you choose Certificate from the main project screen.

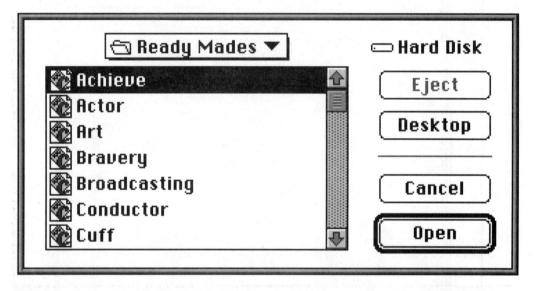

Simply select a certificate, and it is presented on the screen. Then refer to the Certificates Walkthrough on page 50 for directions on modifying a Ready Mades certificate.

Making a Customized Certificate with a Famous Signature.

1. Select Certificate from *The Print Shop Companion* on the Macintosh or from the main menu using Windows.

2. For this activity select a Wide calendar and then from the Landscape backdrop select Blank Page.

3. From the Landscape Layout options, choose Certificate 38 and click OK. This particular layout allows for a Headline Text, Title Block, Seal, and Signature and Rules Lines.

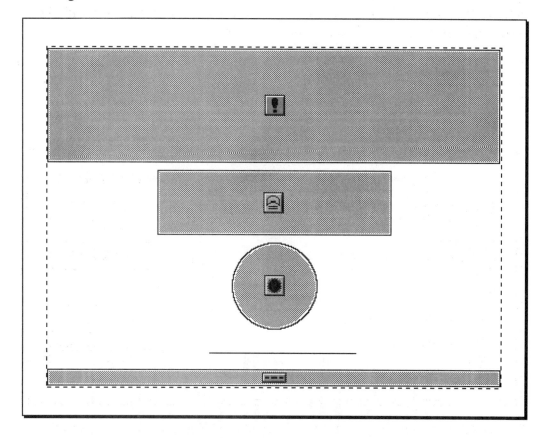

4. Double-click the Headline placeholder and type in your text for the headline.

5. Double-click the Title Block and type in your text.

6. To add a decorative seal to the certificate, double-click the seal, select Seal Center, and choose a center. Select the edge to add a decorative touch.

7. To add a signature, double-click on the signature line and choose the Autograph, color, size, and justification from the Edit Signature screen.

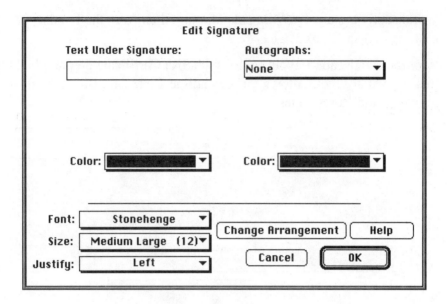

8. Double-click on the rules line at the bottom and choose a line to enhance the certificate.

9. You may also choose a border by selecting Border from the Object menu. Double-click the greyed border and select a graphic.

10. Save and print your certificate.

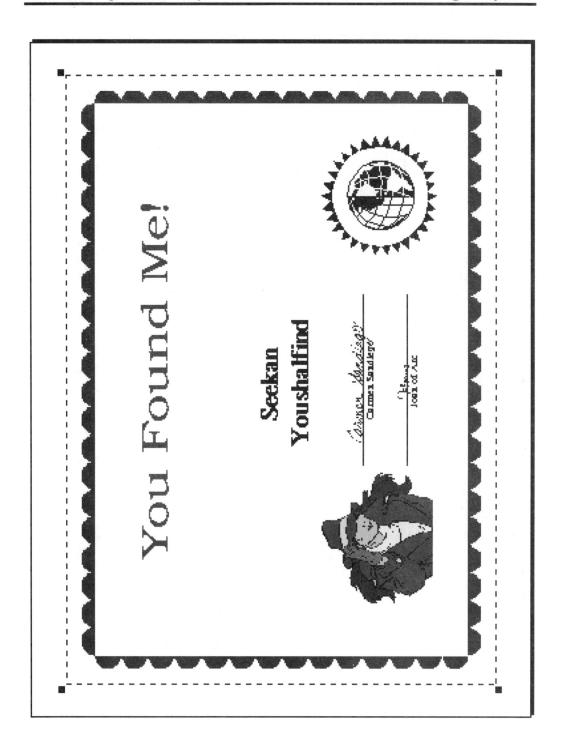

STUDENT PROJECTS INDEX

BANNER FUN

Level: All

Subject Areas: Social Studies, Art, Language Arts

InfoNet: Making banners in connection with the presentation of a class project adds greatly to the visual effect of the presentation. You can make a banner advertising the topic of your presentation with the name and graphics relating to the project on it. For this particular example you are making a banner with the name China and adding appropriate graphics to it.

This Project: Allowing students to create their own personal banners gives them a sense of empowerment because of the professional looks of the banners when they are printed. They can make banners for special events, advertisements for project presentations, school or class elections, etc. Decide with the class which topics they will use as focuses for their banners.

BANNER FUN STUDENT GUIDE

1. Open Banners from the project menu. Select the orientation that you want.

2. The next screen presents choices for Backdrops. For this project choose Blank Page and click OK.

3. The next screen allows you a choice of layouts. Scroll through and see the various layouts possible. For this banner choose Banner 3 and click OK.

4. You see a large display of your banner layout along with the number of pages that will be used.

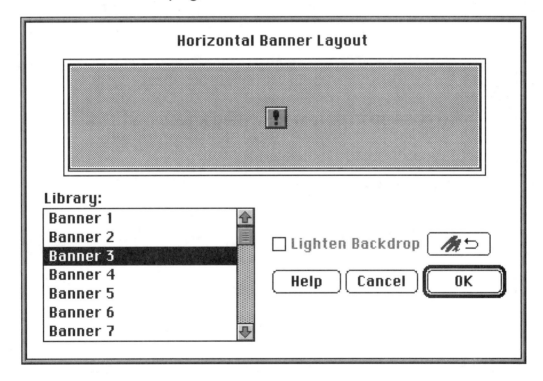

5. Double-click on the Headline placeholder, and you are taken to the Banner Text dialog screen. Type the text that you want. You can change Font, Shape,

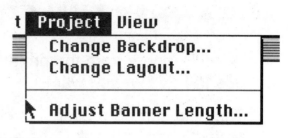

Size and Justify from this screen. If you want to change color, click on Customize and select a color from the palette. If your banner is too small for the graphics that you want to add to it, you can change the size. Select Project and choose Adjust Banner Length. On the next screen change the numbers to larger ones. Highlight the numbers there and type in the new numbers. Click OK. The banner will now have more space between the letters.

Adjust Length of Banner Text Block

Add Leading Space: [1] inches

Add Trailing Space: [8] inches

[Cancel] [OK]

6. To add Square Graphics to the banner, select the Object icon from the tools palette and choose Square Graphic. Double-click on the placeholder and select a graphic. You might need to change libraries. The graphic used in this sample project is from the Square Graphics lebrary named Countries.

7. To change the direction of the graphic, select the graphic by clicking in it once to get the handles. Now, select the Flip Tool in the tool bar, hold down the mouse button, and select Horizontal. You have now flipped the graphic.

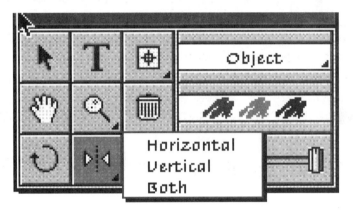

8. Follow the directions above to add more graphics to your banner. When the graphic is placed, resize it by moving the handles diagonally. Move it to where you want it placed and double-click to access the graphics dialog box. Continue in this manner to add more graphics to the banner.

9. When your banner is complete, select Print from the File menu.

What Else Can I Do?

- Create a banner for a classroom event.

ALPHABET CARDS

Level: Primary

Subject Areas: Language Arts, Art

InfoNet: You are going to make a greeting card for an alphabet letter. You put your letter on the front of the card, and on the inside of the card you place pictures of things that start with that letter. You then print the card and place it on the alphabet banner.

This Project: Using the Greeting Card project, students design a card for each letter of the alphabet. It would be best if students could design cards for the first letters of their names, however the x and z might be a little difficult. Before beginning this project, share with students some of the wonderful alphabet books and CD-ROMs available today. You first create a banner with the word "Alphabet" on it. Print the banner and display it at the front of the room. As the students finish their alphabet cards, they place them on the banner. Refer to the teacher walkthrough section on making a banner for directions.

You will need to model the following instructions for the students before they start.

ALPHABET CARDS STUDENT GUIDE

1. Open the Greeting Card project from the main menu and choose Top Fold.

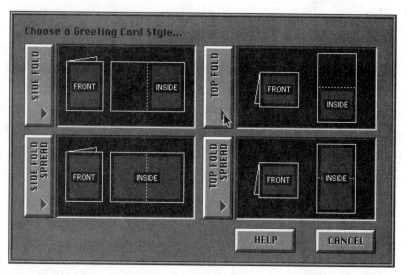

2. Choose Blank Page in the Landscape Backdrop screen. Click OK.

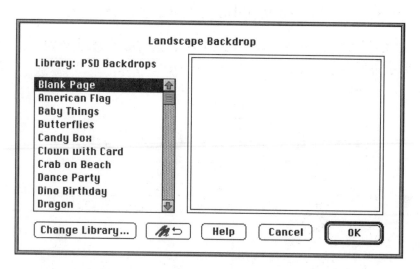

3. The next screen is where you choose the layout or the way the card is designed. For this card, you want a large space where you can type in your letter. Greeting Card 3 on the Macintosh gives you that space. If you are using the Windows version, look through the choices for a layout that has the large text area. Click OK.

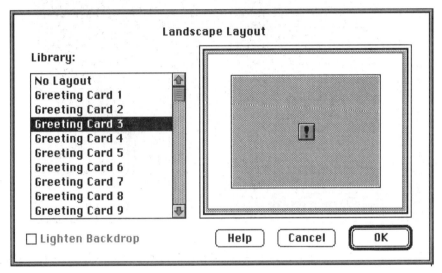

4. You now have a screen that shows the layout.

5. Double-click on the middle of the screen and you now see a Headline Text box. Here is where you type in your letter.

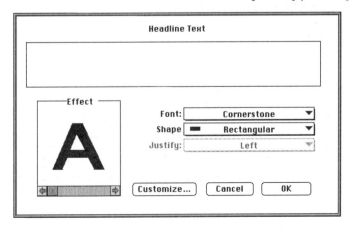

6. Type in your letter. Macintosh: To make your letter in color, click on the button that says Customize at the bottom of the screen.

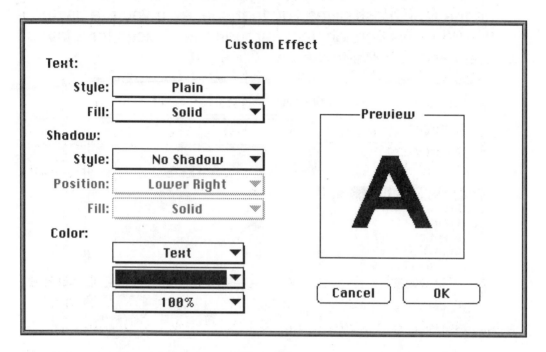

This takes you to a screen where you can add color to your letter. Look for the word "Color," hold down on the mouse button with the arrow on the color menu and then choose the color that you want. Click OK and you are back to a screen that shows your letter on the front of a greeting card. Windows: The color choice can be made from the Headline Edit screen.

7. Let's add a border to the front of the card. Since the card already shows a grey border, you just have to double-click on the grey border. You now have a choice of borders to put on your card. Click OK when you find the border you want.

8. Now we need to get to the inside of the card. Select Project from the menu bar, hold down the mouse, and choose Inside of Card.

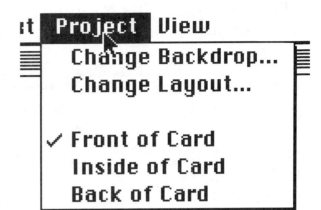

9. Choose Blank Page from the Landscape Backdrop box and click OK. Then click OK again for the Landscape Layout choice. You now have a blank card on which to put pictures.

10. To place a picture:

   • Macintosh: Click on the Object icon in the Tool Palette and move your mouse to Square Graphic. On your screen a Square Graphic Placeholder appears.

   • Windows: Select Graphic from the menu bar at the left side of the screen.

10. Double-click on the Square Graphic placeholder and choose a graphic that begins with your letter. Select the graphic and click OK.

   If there is not a graphic that you need in the ones shown on the screen, you can choose to browse through other libraries. Macintosh: Click on the Change Library button. Windows: Browse through the libraries listed on the screen.

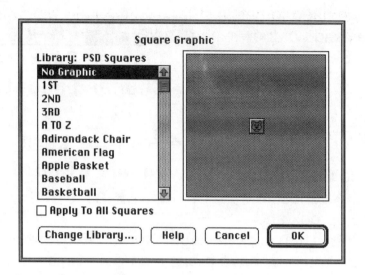

If you choose a graphic and you don't like it, press delete. If the handles are not around the graphic, click once and they will appear; then press delete.

12. You can make the graphic larger or smaller by moving the mouse to one of the handles and pulling it out or pushing it in.

13. You can move your graphic by putting the mouse arrow in the middle of the graphic, holding down the mouse button and moving the mouse. If the graphic doesn't move, click once. The handles will appear which means that you can move it.

14. Keep adding graphics just the way you did with the first one. When you are finished adding graphics, it is time to print.

15. Select File from the menu bar and choose Print. This will print the card. After it is printed, fold and trim. Now put it on the alphabet banner.

Now What Else Can I Do?

- Animal cards
- Science cards
- Students cards

HOLIDAY GREETING CARD

Level: Primary

Subject Areas: Language Arts, Art

InfoNet: You are going to make a greeting card for Thanksgiving or another holiday. You choose the graphics, font types, and borders and write whatever you want using the Greeting Card project.

This Project: Using the Greeting Card project, students each design a card to give to important persons in their lives. In selecting the graphics, students' knowledge of the holiday is reinforced by making the correct choices.

You will need to model the following instructions for the students before they start.

GREETING CARD STUDENT GUIDE

1. Open the Greeting Card project from the main menu and choose Top Fold.

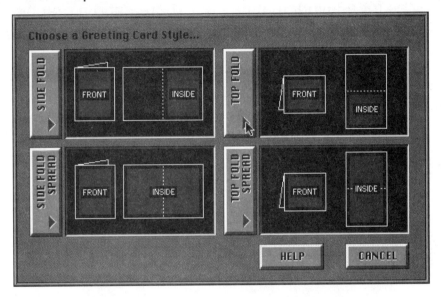

2. Choose Blank Page in the Landscape Backdrop screen. Click OK.

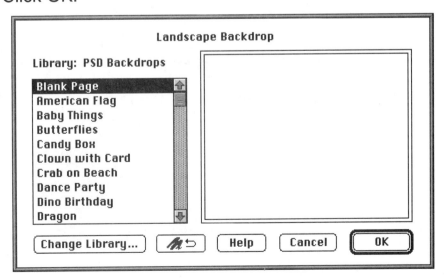

3. The next screen is where you choose the layout or the way the front of the card is designed. Greeting Card 9 on the Macintosh gives you space for graphics and greetings. If you are using the Windows version, look through the choices for a layout that has a text area and a graphic area. Click OK.

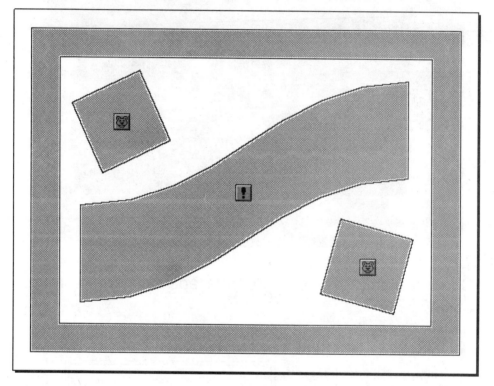

4. You now have a screen that shows the layout.

5. Double-click on the middle of the screen, and you see a Headline Text box. It has an exclamation mark in it.

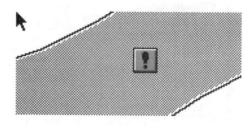

Here is where you type in your greeting.

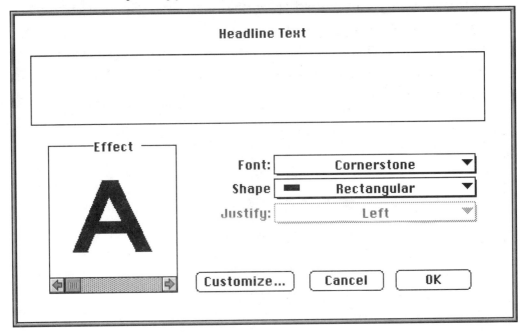

6. Type in your greeting, "Happy Thanksgiving."

- Macintosh: To make your letter in color, click on the button that says Customize at the bottom of the screen. This takes you to a screen where you can add color to your letter. Just look for the word Color, hold down the color arrow, and move the mouse to the color you want. Click OK, and you are back to a screen that shows your greeting on the front of a greeting card.

- Windows: The color choice can be made from the Headline Edit screen.

7. Let's add a border to the front of the card. Since the card already shows a grey border, you just have to double-click on the grey border. You now have a choice of borders to put on your card.

Click on each border once to see how it looks in the preview window. Click OK when you find the border you want.

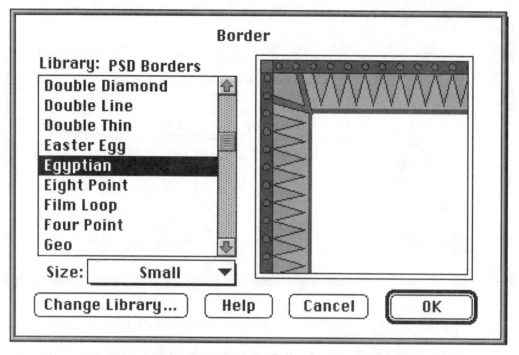

8. Now it is time to put the graphic on your card front. Double-click on the Square Graphic Placeholder and choose a graphic for your card. You might need to use the Change Library button to find more graphics.

9. When you find a graphic that you want, click OK. Double-click in any other Graphic placeholders and place graphics just like you did in step 8.

10. Now we need to go to the inside of the card. Select Project from the menu bar, hold down the mouse, and choose Inside of Card.

11. Choose Blank Card from the Landscape Backdrop and No Layout from the Landscape Layout screen. You now have a blank card on which to put text and graphics.

12. To place a picture:

    • Macintosh: Click on the Object icon in the Tool Palette and move your mouse to Square Graphic. A Square Graphic placeholder appears on your screen. Move the placeholder to any part of the screen that you want by placing the mouse arrow in the middle of the placeholder and moving your mouse. Choose your graphic by following the directions in Step 9.

    • Windows: Select Graphic from the left side of the screen. There on your screen a Square Graphic placeholder appears. Move the placeholder to any part of the screen that you want by placing the mouse arrow in the middle of the placeholder and moving your mouse.

13. Double-click on the Square Graphic Placeholder and choose a graphic that shows Thanksgiving and click OK. If there is not a graphic that you need in the ones shown on the screen, you can choose to browse through other libraries.

    • Macintosh: Click on the Change Library button.

    • Windows: Browse through the libraries listed on the screen.

If after you choose a graphic you don't like, press delete. If the handles are not around the graphic, click once and they will appear; then press delete.

14. You can make the graphic larger or smaller by moving the mouse to one of the handles and pulling it out or pushing it in.

15. You can move your graphic by putting the mouse arrow in the middle of the graphic, holding down the mouse button and moving the mouse. If the graphic doesn't move, click once, and the handles will appear, and then you can move it.

16. Keep adding graphics just the way you did the first one. When you are finished adding graphics, it is time to print.

17. Select File from the menu bar and choose Print. This will print the card. After it is printed, fold and trim it.

Thanksgiving is a time to give thanks for the things we have. I am thankful for you. Love, Cindy

Now What Else Can I Do?

- Make Mother's Day, Father's Day, graduation, Christmas, Fourth of July, Kwanzaa, Hanukkah, birthday, Halloween cards, and many more. The graphics for all of these holidays and special occasions are available.

LETTER BOOKS

Level: Primary

Subject Areas: Language Arts

InfoNet: Choose the letters of the alphabet that you want to illustrate. Look through the Graphics book to find pictures you can use. For this project you are going to work on the letter B.

This Project: In this project students create their own letter books, either for themselves or to share with lower grade students. The project can be created in English or in other languages. This project is designed for younger children and introduces them to several elements in *The Print Shop*. Before they work on the computer, students pre-plan their work by choosing pictures that begin with specific letters of the alphabet. Use the extensive book that accompanies *The Print Shop* program.

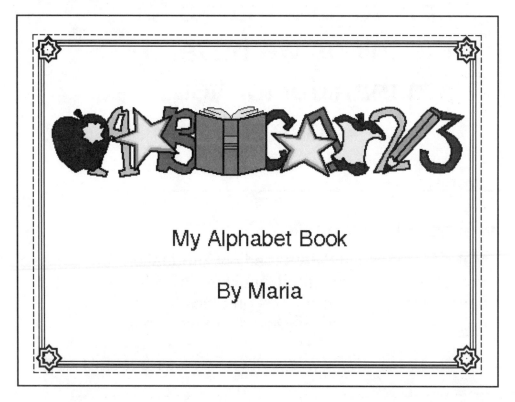

LETTER BOOKS STUDENT GUIDE

1. Open the Sign project from the main menu and choose Wide Orientation.

2. Choose Blank Page from the Backdrop screen and click OK.

3. The next screen is where you choose the layout or the way the page is designed. For this project, choose No Layout and click OK.

4. You now have a screen that shows a page that is ready for you to design.

5. To write your alphabet letter, select the text tool by clicking on it. Move your mouse to the blank page and draw a text box for your letter on the upper left-hand part of the screen.

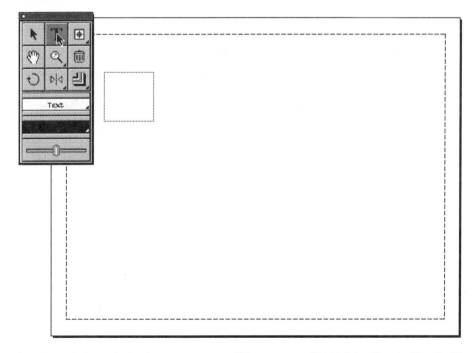

6. Type in the letter B. Type in the letter both in capital and lowercase. To make a capital, press down the shift key and press the letter.

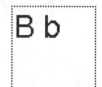

7. Now let's add a picture that starts with a B. Select Object from the Tool Palette and choose Square Graphic. You now have a placeholder for a Square Graphic. Double-click on the placeholder, and you have a list of graphics on the screen. Hold down the arrow at the right side of the list of graphics until you come to one that starts with B. Click on the graphic title and press OK. You now have the graphic on the screen.

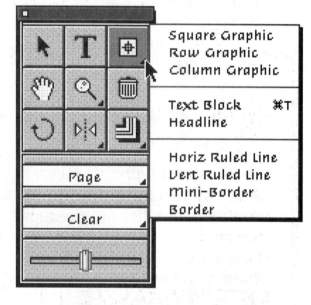

8. Now repeat the directions in number 7 to place more graphics on your page. When you select another graphic and it is placed on the screen, it may not be in the place where you want it. To move it, click in the center of the graphic, hold down the mouse button, and move it to where you want it.

It will only move if the handles are showing around it. To get the handles, click once in the middle of the graphic.

9. If you need a graphic that is not on the graphic list, you can find some more graphics by selecting Change Libraries at the bottom of the screen. Look for other libraries that have graphics you want. When you find one, double-click on the name and it will appear on your screen.

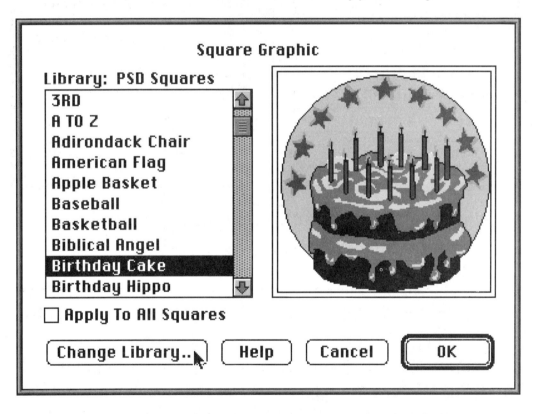

10. Now let's add a border to the page. Select the Object icon and then choose Border. You now have a greyed-out area on the screen. Double-click in the greyed-out area and choose a border.

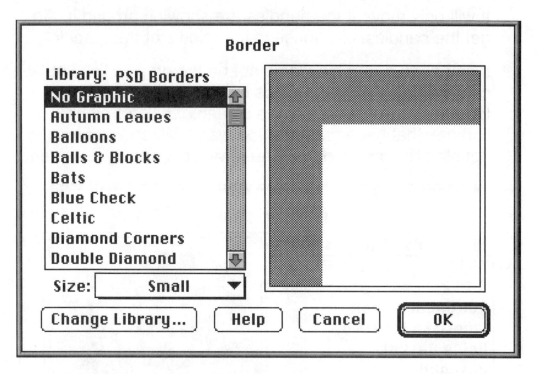

11. When you are ready to print, select Print from the file menu and print your work.

What Else Can I Do?

- Create an alphabet page for every letter of the alphabet.

- Create an alphabet page showing each letter of your name.

- Staple the pages together for your own book. Use the Sign project to make a cover for your alphabet book.

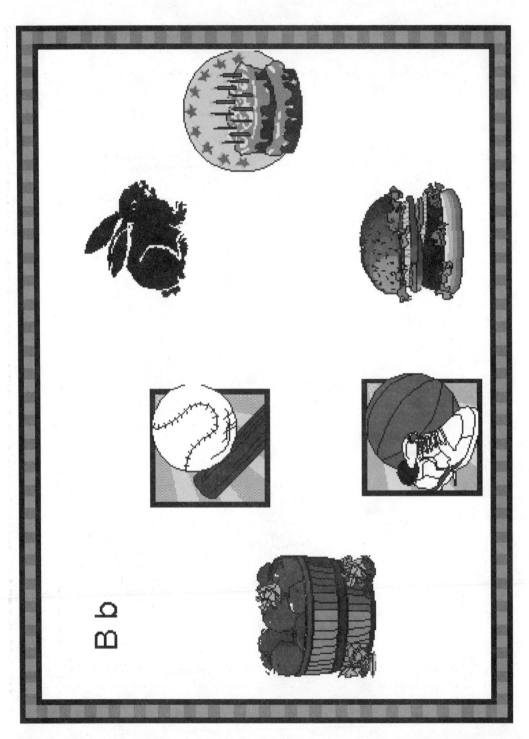

B b

NUMBER BOOKS

Level: Primary

Subject Areas: Language Arts, Math

InfoNet: This project is for you to create a book about numbers. On each page you write the numeral and the number word. You then choose a graphic for the number and repeat the graphic as many times as needed.

This Project: In this project students create their own number books either for themselves or to share with lower grade students. The project can be created in English or other languages. This project is designed for younger children and introduces them to several elements in *The Print Shop*. Before they work on the computer, students pre-plan their work by writing a number on paper and writing the number word next to it. Use the extensive book that accompanies *The Print Shop* program.

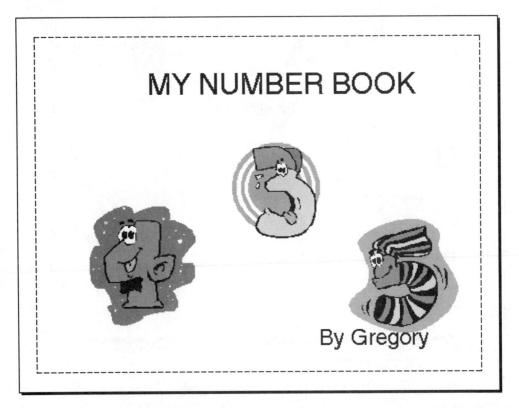

NUMBER BOOKS STUDENT GUIDE

1. Open the Sign project from the main menu and choose Wide Orientation.

2. Choose Blank Page from the Backdrop screen and click OK.

3. The next screen is where you choose the layout or the way the page is designed. For this project, choose No Layout and click OK.

4. You now have a screen that shows a page that is ready for you to design.

5. To write your number, select the Text Tool by clicking on it. Move your mouse to the blank page and draw a text box for your letter on the upper left-hand part of the screen.

6. Type in the number 1. Press the space bar two times. Write the word one. If the text box is too small, click on the Pointer Tool in the Tool Palette and then click in the text box. Pull one of the handles out.

7. Now let's add a picture of one item. Select Object from the Tool Palette and choose Square Graphic. You now have a placeholder, for a Square Graphic. Double-click on the placeholder and you have a list of graphics on the screen. Hold down the arrow at the right side of the list of graphics until you come to one that has one object. Click on the graphic title and press OK. You now have the graphic on the screen.

8. Now let's add a border to the page. Select the Object icon and then choose Border. You now have a greyed-out area on the screen. Double-click in the greyed-out area and choose a border.

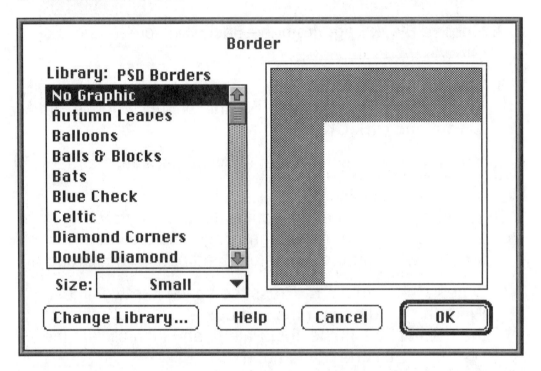

9. If your teacher directs you to save the picture before you print, select File and then choose Save. Name your picture and be sure to add your initials.

10. When you are ready to print, select Print from the File menu and print your work.

11. Now you are ready to create a page for the number 2. Follow the directions in Numbers 1–7 except enter number 2 and the word two and so on. After you have placed a graphic of one item, you are now going to repeat that item to make two.

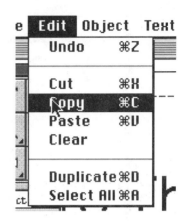

12. The handles should be around the graphic. If not, click on the graphic. When the handles are around the graphic, select Edit and then choose Copy.

13. Click on the screen where you want the next picture. Select Edit again and choose the word Paste.

    Hold your mouse arrow over the new addition and move it to where you want it.

Add the border and print.

What Else Can I Do?

- Create a number page for many different numbers.
- Staple the pages together for your own book.
- Use the Sign Project to make a cover for your number book.

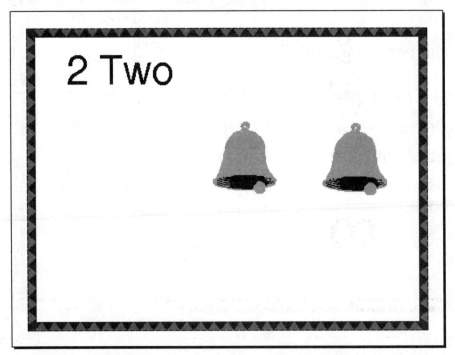

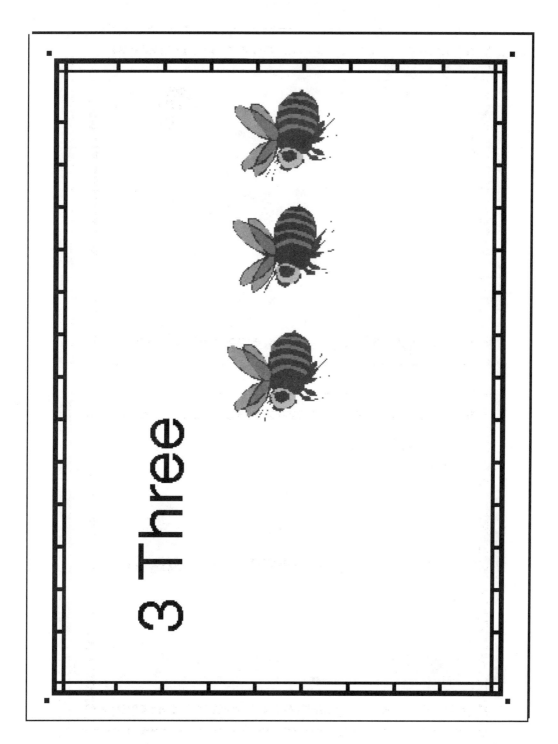

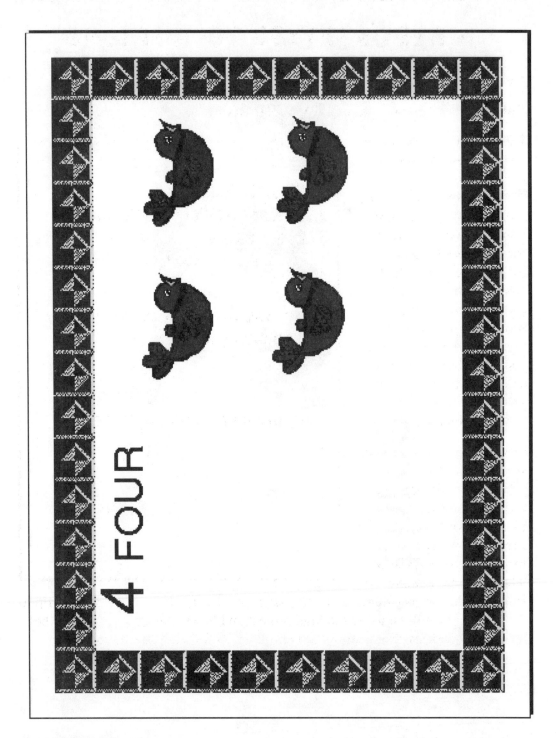

4 FOUR

A REBUS LETTER TO A FRIEND

Level: Primary

Subject Areas: Language Arts, Art, Social Studies

InfoNet: It's really fun to write a mystery letter to a friend. To make it a mystery, you will be using words for only part of the letter. The other part of the letter is written with pictures. This is called rebus writing. In this project, you will write a rebus letter to a friend, pretending that you have just visited the zoo. You should write the draft of your letter first before you use the computer.

This Project: Review with students the concept of a rebus story. Explain that rebus pictures take the place of words and that the reader has to replace the rebus pictures with words when they are reading the story. In this project students create a letter to a friend about an imaginary trip to the zoo. They will be using the Sign project and Square Graphics. It might be better if students write the drafts of their letters before they use the computer.

Dear Chuck,
    Last week I went to the zoo. I saw a

He was black and white. I also saw two

My favorite animal was the

        Your friend,
        Joe

You will need to model the following instructions for the students before they begin.

A REBUS LETTER TO A FRIEND STUDENT GUIDE

1. Open the Sign project from the main menu and choose Tall.

2. Choose Blank Page in the Portrait Backdrop screen. Click OK.

3. The next screen is where you choose the layout or the way the letter is designed. For this project, choose No Layout and press OK.

4. You now have a screen that shows a page that is blank.

5. You are now going to write your letter. Click on the Text Tool icon in the Tools Palette. Click on the screen towards the top and pull diagonally towards the bottom right. This makes the area in which you write your letter.

6. In the upper left-hand corner you see a flashing cursor. This is where you begin your writing. Write your sentence and leave space where you want your graphic to be placed.

7. Select the Object icon in the Tool Palette and choose the Square Graphic. On your screen is a Placeholder with four handles around it. Put your mouse arrow in the middle of the placeholder and move it to the bottom of the screen.

Now, double-click on the placeholder. You now get to choose a graphic for the square. If there is not a graphic listed that you want, select Change Libraries and select a graphic from another library. Double-click on the graphic you want. It then appears on your screen.

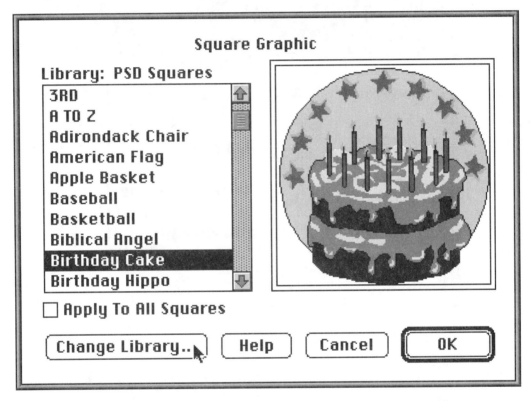

8. If it appears too small, hold down your mouse arrow on one of the handles and pull it out slightly.

9. Let's add another picture to the page now. Repeat steps 6 and 7. When the placeholder appears on the screen, move it to where you need the picture. If you put in a picture you don't want, click on it to get the handles and then press the delete key. The picture disappears.

10. Let's add a border for the letter. Select the Object icon from the Tool Palette and choose Border. You now have a greyed-out area around the page. Double-click on the grey area and choose a border for the text on the screen.

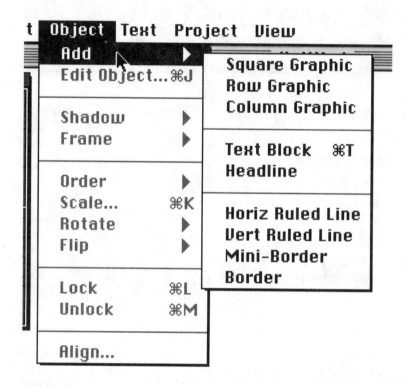

11. When you are ready to print, select Print from the File menu and print your work.

What Else Can I Do?

- Write rebus letters about many different subject areas. Dinosaurs make a good subject for a letter.

Dear Mom and Dad,

   We are learning about dinosaurs. Today we learned about the

   Mrs. Smith, our teacher, says that we will also learn about

Did you know that dinosaurs did not eat people because there were no people alive then?

   Your favorite son,

                    Billy

MY BIRTHDAY MONTH

Level: Primary–Intermediate

Subject Area: Language Arts and Technology

InfoNet: Having a birthday party is fun for everyone involved, but it takes planning to have a successful event. Making a calendar on which you show the dates that certain projects need to be completed helps you to use your time wisely in planning your party.

This Project: Students design and print calendars for their birthday months. They note the dates on which they need to make and then send their party invitations. They note the dates on which they need to shop for their party goods and foods. This project helps students learn to plan future events and to allocate time.

Before the Computer: Think of the date on which you want to have your party. Check with a parent to see if that is convenient. Decide who is going to be invited, what will be served, and what other items you need for the party. Decide on days by which things will be finished.

MY BIRTHDAY MONTH STUDENT GUIDE

1. Open the Calendar project from the main menu screen. Choose the Monthly Calendar Type from the next screen.

2. So that the calendar will fit in your notebook, choose the Tall Orientation from the next screen.

3. On the next screen use the arrow to choose a year and click on your birthday month. Click OK.

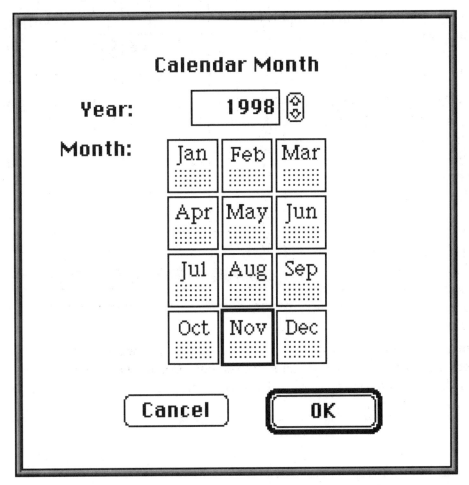

4. On the next screen, click on the Blank Page choice.

5. Now you can choose a layout for your calendar. This example uses Calendar 3. Click OK.

6. You are now shown the calendar with the month and year.

7. Now let's place the graphics for your calendar. Double-click on the Square Graphic placeholder and choose a graphic to place. If you want to have all the graphics on the calendar the same, click on the Apply to All Squares box at the bottom of the screen.

8. To write and illustrate in the various date squares, simply double-click in the date square, and the next screen shows the Edit Calendar Day dialog box.

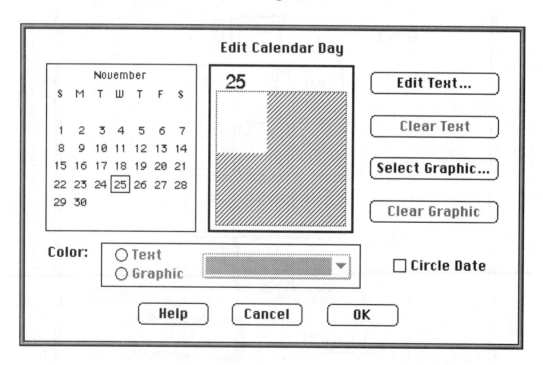

9. If you want a graphic in your date box, you should place it in the box first and then write the text over it. To do this, select the Select Graphic button from the dialog box. Now choose a graphic from the list presented and click OK.

10. To write the text, choose Edit Text, and then you can write in your text. Type in the text that you want. You can make changes from this screen also. You can change font, size, and color from this screen. Remember that to make changes you must highlight the text so that the computer knows what you want to change.

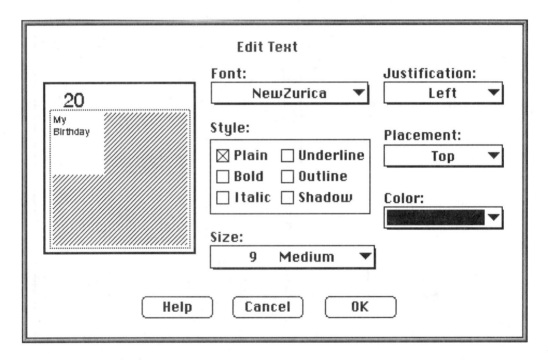

- Hold down the arrow in the Font section and choose a different font by just moving the mouse arrow over to it.

- Change the color by holding down the mouse arrow on the color arrow and moving to the color you want.

- Change the font size by moving the mouse arrow to the arrow in the size selection area and choosing a size.

  When the text is how you want it, click OK, and you are taken back to the Edit Calendar Day dialog box. There you can choose another date box to edit, or if you are finished, click OK.

11. To add a border to your calendar, select Object from the menu bar and choose Border. Select the border you want and click OK.

12. To print your document, select Print from the File menu.

What Else Can I Do?

- Make calendars for important school events, sporting events, and homework.

- Make calendars for historic events. This is great for class reports.

MATH STORIES

Level: Primary-Intermediate

Subject Areas: Language Arts, Art, Math

InfoNet: In this project you use your imagination and creativity to write and publish story problems for math. There are many choices of graphics that you can use, so it should be fun creating your own math problems for classmates to solve. You might even write some story problems for younger students to solve. You will want to write your story first before you use the computer. You probably will want to add some quick sketches of your graphic choices too. This example is an easy addition story problem.

This Project: Writing and solving math story problems has often been difficult for students. By

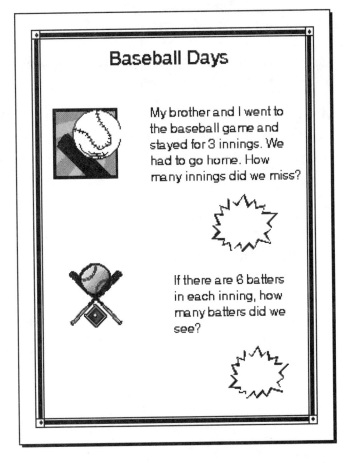

using the capabilities of *The Print Shop* projects, students will be able to include graphics and use different fonts for their story problems, thus making it a little easier to be creative in their writing. This project is especially timely for the middle elementary grades, but lower elementary grade students will benefit from the project greatly with a little bit of modeling. Have students write their stories first and sketch in their graphics before they use the computer.

MATH STORIES STUDENT GUIDE

1. Open the Sign project from the main menu and choose Tall Orientation.

2. Choose Blank Page from the next menu. Choose No Layout and click OK.

3. You now have a screen that shows a page that is ready for you to create your story problem.

4. Let's put the graphic in first. Select Object from the Tool palette and choose Square Graphic. Move the graphic placeholder to the left side of the page. Double-click on the placeholder and choose your graphic.

5. To write text next to the graphic, select the Text Tool from the Object menu and draw a text box next to the graphic.

One day I was walking down the street eating my apple when another apple fell out of a tree and landed at my feet.

6. Now type in the text.

7. If the size of the font is too large for the box, highlight the text and choose Size from the Text menu.

Select a smaller size and write your text. You can also click on the Pointer Tool in the Tool Palette and then click on the text box. You can then move the handles of the text box so that the box is bigger and the text fits inside of it.

8. Add a second graphic and text box for your math story.

9. Let's add a border. Select the Object icon from the Tool Palette and choose Border. You now have a greyed-out area around the page. Double-click on the grey area and choose a border.

10. If you want to have an area on the page which someone could use to solve the problem with an illustration, add a mini-border for that small area. Select Object and choose Mini-Border.

11. When you are ready to print, select Print from the File menu and print your work.

What Else Can I Do?

- Write math story problems for all of the operations: addition, subtraction, multiplication, division.

An Apple a Day

One day I was walking down the street eating my apple when another apple fell out of a tree and landed at my feet.

I now had two apples. Mom says that it takes 10 apples to make an apple pie. How many more do I need?

$2+?=10$

Draw the answer here>>>>

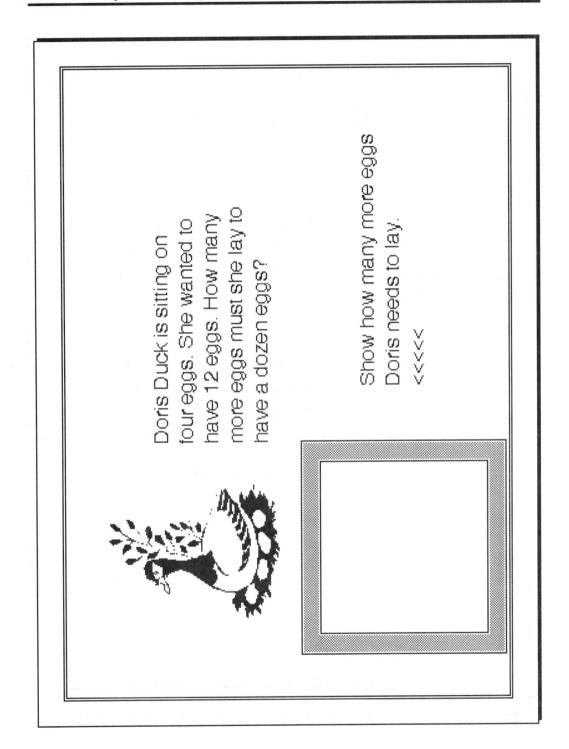

Doris Duck is sitting on four eggs. She wanted to have 12 eggs. How many more eggs must she lay to have a dozen eggs?

Show how many more eggs Doris needs to lay.

Olympics

Lita got 8 points on the balance beam. Tina got 6 points. Judy got 5 points. What was the average number of points for the balance beam?

Tom can lift 200 lbs. Mike can lift 237 lbs. Alan can lift 275 lbs. What is the average weight these 3 men lift?

Do your work here.

COLORFUL STORIES

Level: Primary–Intermediate

Subject Areas: Language Arts, Art

InfoNet: It's always fun to write stories. It is even more fun to write them on backgrounds that are colorful. You are going to write a story with some wonderful graphics in the background.

For this project, you are going to write a story about a gingerbread man.

This Project: Using the artwork from *The Print Shop*, students write their own stories against a related backdrop. You might want to preview a related backdrops with the students and list suggestions on the board as to story possibilities for each backdrop.

You will need to model the following instructions for the students before they begin.

COLORFUL STORIES STUDENT GUIDE

1. Open the Sign project from the main menu and choose Tall.

2. Choose Gingerbread Man in the Portrait Backdrop screen. Click OK.

3. The next screen is where you choose the layout or the way the project is designed. For this project, choose No Layout and press OK.

4. You now have a screen that shows a page that has a border and a picture of a gingerbread man.

5. Now we need to write the story. Select the Text Tool from the Tool Palette. Move your mouse over to the page, click at the top left-hand corner and drag diagonally to make an area where you can write.

6. You see a cursor in the upper left hand corner. Type in your story. Be sure to keep your story in the text box. If it goes outside of the box, it will not print. If it does not fit, highlight the text and choose a smaller size from the Text menu.

7. Let's add a border for the story. Select the Object icon from the Tool Palette and choose Border. You now have a greyed-out area around the page. Double-click on the grey area and choose a border for text on the screen.

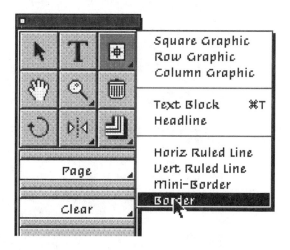

8. When you are ready to print, select Print from the File menu and print your work.

What Else Can I Do?

• Write stories about different subjects: Halloween, Easter, Kites, A Good Lunch, Ocean and Jungle, Sandcastles, St. Patrick's Day, A Snowy Day, A Moon Landing, etc.

Birds

There are over 9,000 different species of birds. They have adapted to survive in almost every environment around the world. They live in the desert and in the cities. They live in the mountains and in the arctic.

Halloween is lots of fun. We get to dress up in costumes and go Trick or Treating. My Mom makes my costume. This year I want to be a pirate.

Japanese Boy's Day

In Japan there is a holiday for boys. On that day the boys hang kites in front of their homes. If there is room, they fly them high in the sky.

ME, MYSELF, AND I MOBILE

Level: Primary–Intermediate

Subject Areas: Language Arts, Art, Social Studies

InfoNet: You are going to make a mobile that shows all about you. It shows your favorite foods, sports, and family members. You first choose pictures that tell about you and then print and cut out the pictures. The last step is to put string on the pictures and hang them from a hanger or stick to create a mobile.

This Project: Students are asked to think about all the things that are unique and important to them. They focus on their family life and school life and personal feelings. Using the Sign project, they write a title for their mobile and import graphics into the Sign Project. After this is complete, they print and cut out the graphics and attach string to them. They then tie the strings to a hanger for a mobile.

You will need to model the following instructions for the students before they begin.

ME, MYSELF, AND I MOBILE STUDENT GUIDE

1. Open the Sign project from the main menu and choose Tall.

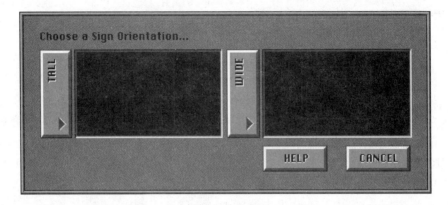

2. Choose Blank Page in the Portrait Backdrop screen. Click OK.

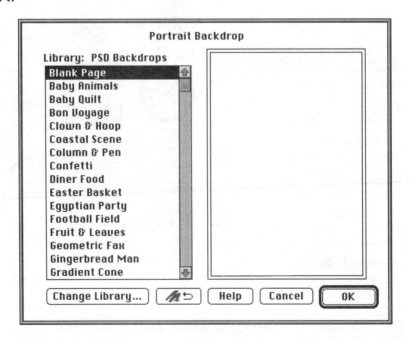

3. The next screen is where you choose the layout or the way the sign is designed. For this project, choose No Layout and press OK.

4. You now have a screen that shows a page that is blank.

5. You are now going to choose your pictures. Click on the Object icon in the Tools Palette, and choose the Square Graphic.

6. On your screen is a placeholder with four handles around it. Put your mouse arrow in the middle of the square and move it to the bottom left of the screen. Now, double-click on the placeholder. You now get to choose a graphic for the square. If there is not a graphic listed that you want, select Change Libraries and select a graphic from another library. Double-click on the graphic you want, and it then appears on your screen.

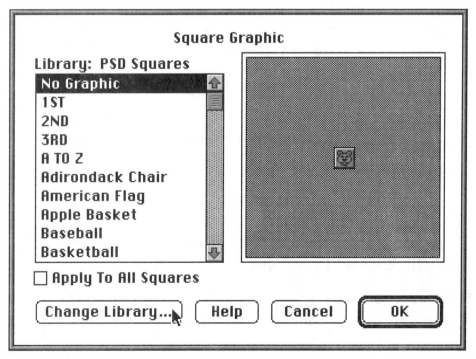

7. If it appears too small, hold down your mouse arrow on one of the handles and pull it out slightly.

8. Let's add another picture to the page now. Repeat Steps 5, 6, and 7. When the placeholder appears on the screen, move it to the right-hand corner. If you put in a picture you don't want, click on it to get the handles and then press the delete key. The picture disappears.

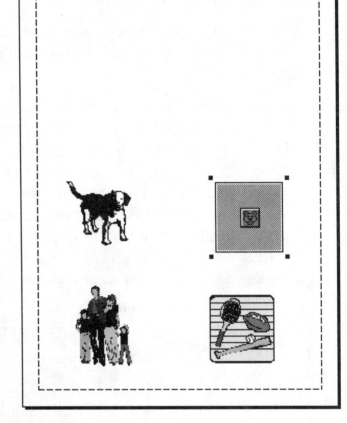

9. Keep adding pictures to your screen until you have at least six pictures on the screen.

10. Let's add a title for the mobile. Select the Object icon from the Tool Palette and choose Headline. You now have a placeholder for text on the screen. Double-click on the placeholder and write in your text. Click OK.

11. When you are ready to print, select Print from the File menu and print your work.

12. Cut out the graphics and the title. Punch a hole at the top of each graphic and tie string or yarn to the graphic.

13. Use many different lengths of string or yarn. Punch a hole at each corner of the title and tie the string or yarn to it.

14. Attach the string or yarn to a hanger or stick, and there you have your mobile.

Now What Else Can I Do?

- Holiday Mobiles: Thanksgiving, Halloween, Christmas

- History Mobile: Independence Day, Columbus Day

- Food Mobile: Breakfast

A Good Breakfast

Columbus Day

Independence Day

LITERARY LETTERHEAD AND LETTERS

Level: Intermediate–Challenging

Subject Areas: Language Arts, Art

InfoNet: Think about characters in books that you have read either in school or at home. Pretend that you are that person and imagine to whom you would write a letter and what you would say in the letter. You should write the draft of your letter before you use the computer. For this example you are going to write a letter from the giant's mother to Jack's mother.

This Project: Using the Letterhead project, children create letterhead and stationery upon which they each write as if they were a literary character. This is a wonderful project to use as the culmination of a literary study. Have students think about what their characters would say in a letter and to whom they would write. It is best if students write a draft of their letter before using the computer.

You will need to model the following instructions for the students before they begin.

Fee, Fi, Fo Fum Castle

Gertrude Giant
Mulberry, England

Dear Jack's mother,

    I have been meaning to write you for some time about your son, Jack. My husband, Mr. Giant, has asked him repeatedly not to return to our castle. And yet, he constantly climbs the beanstalk to our home. Now I agree that Jack is a nice fellow, and he does have a hearty appetite. There is one problem though; he tends to take things that are not his. We are missing several items, including our golden harp and our special goose. Please talk with him about this.

        Regards,
        Mrs. Giant

LITERARY LETTERHEAD AND LETTERS STUDENT GUIDE

1. Open the Letterhead project from the main menu screen and choose Tall. Choose Single size from the Letterhead size screen.

2. Choose Notebook in the Portrait Backdrop screen. Click OK.

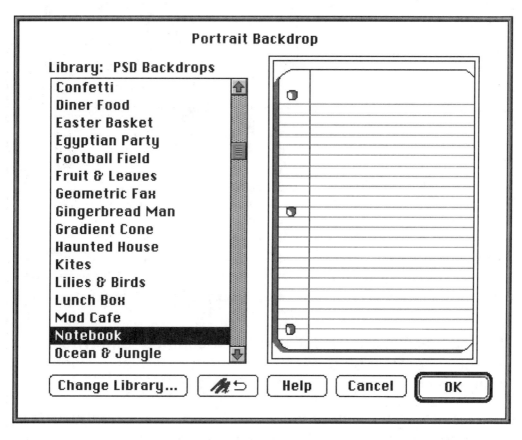

3. The next screen is where you choose the layout or the way the letter is designed. For this project, choose Notebook 1 and click OK.

4. You now have a screen that shows a page that looks like a notebook page with two Placeholders. One placeholder is for the letterhead, and the other is for the text.

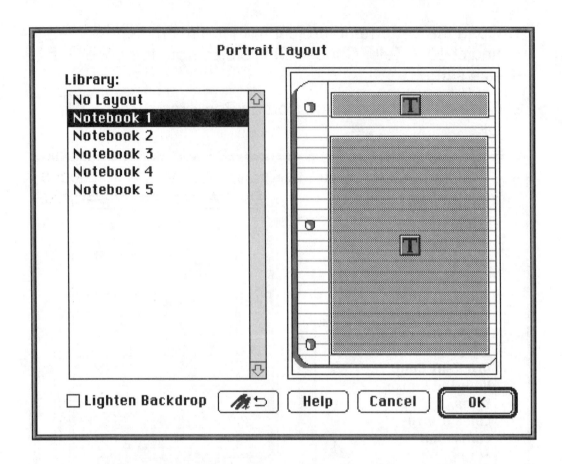

5. Double-click on the Letterhead placeholder and type in your character's address. If the font is too large, highlight it and choose Size from the Text menu.

· 6. You are now going to write your letter. Click on the Text placeholder. This is the area in which you write your letter.

7. In the upper left-hand corner you see a flashing cursor. This is where you begin your writing. Write your sentence and leave space where you want your graphic to be placed.

If you want to place a graphic with your text, select the Object icon in the Tool Palette and choose the Square Graphic. On your screen is a placeholder with four handles around it. Put your mouse arrow in the middle of the placeholder and move it to the bottom of the screen. Now, double-click on the placeholder. You now get to choose a graphic for the square. If there is not a graphic listed that you want, select Change Libraries and select a graphic from another library. Double-click on the graphic you want, and it then appears on your screen.

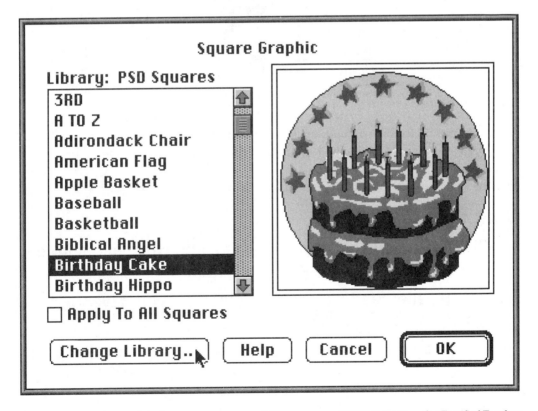

If it appears too large or small, hold down your mouse arrow on one of the handles and pull it in or out slightly.

8. Let's add a border for the letter. Select the Object icon from the Tool Palette and choose Border. You now have a greyed-out area around the page. Double-click on the grey area and choose a border for text on the screen.

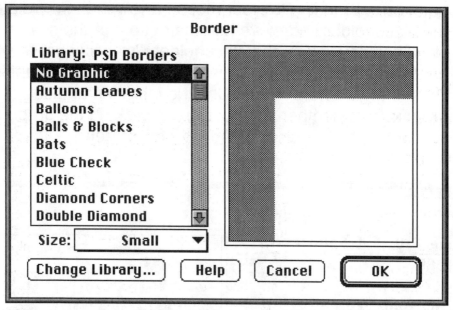

9. When you are ready to print, select Print from the File menu and print your work.

What Else Can I Do?

- Choose famous cartoon characters and write letters from them to your friends.

- Create letterhead and write a letter from your favorite sports person to a friend.

- Create letterhead and write a letter from a historical figure.

A PIECE OF HISTORY

Level: Intermediate–Challenging

Subject Areas: Language Arts, History

InfoNet: Complete your research on the material for the newsletter. Write a draft copy of the text before you work at the computer. Pretend that you are living at the time that the events in the newsletter take place. It is always a good practice to picture the person for whom you are writing. In this case, because it is a historical newsletter, think of the reader dressed as people did in the period about which you are writing. For this particular example you are writing a newsletter from long ago.

This Project: By creating a newsletter as if they lived in a particular historical period, students are able to use their research in a unique manner. This project can also be used for creating newsletters related to current events. It is very easy to do this project in pairs. The students research a historical period and then create a newsletter related to their research. The pre-computer work should also include a draft copy of the text of the newsletter.

The AthensTimes
420 B.C.

The Acropolis

Erechtheum, the new temple is open to the public. It is constructed on the site of the contest between Poseidon and Athene. Visit today!

Drama Festival

To honor the god Dionysus, a drama festival will be held in the Odeon concert hall tomorrow. Buy your tickets at the Athens Hot Tix office at 113 Olive St.

A PIECE OF HISTORY
STUDENT GUIDE

1. Open the Sign project from the main menu and choose Tall Orientation.

2. Choose Blank Page from the Backdrop screen.

3. The next screen is where you choose the Layout or the way the sign is designed. For this project, choose Sign Layout 16 or 18 and press OK.

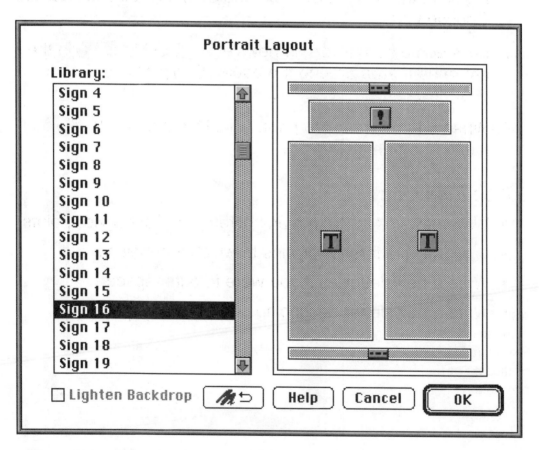

4. You now have a screen that shows a page that is formatted with two columns and a headline or masthead. Double-click on the Headline placeholder and type in the title of the newsletter. Click OK when you are finished.

5. Double-click on the Text placeholder and write your text. If the size of the font is too large, highlight and choose Size from the text menu. Select a smaller size and write your text.

6. If the text is centered and you want it left justified, highlight the text, select Text and then choose Justification. Choose Left.

7. Let's add a border for the newsletter. Double-click on the greyed-out area around the page. Choose a border for your newsletter.

8. When you are ready to print, select Print from the File menu and print your work.

What Else Can I Do?

- Write newsletters from many different historical viewpoints.
- Write newsletters for groups to which you belong.
- Write a newsletter as if you were in outer space.
- Write a newsletter describing classroom activities.

Animal Gazette

Beauty Contest

Thursday the elephant group will hold their annual contest for nose length. Trunks will be measured and prizes awarded. Only elephants need apply as they are the only animals in the order called proboscids.

Family Facts

A herd of African elephants is made up of a number of small family groups. Each group has a female, and her young sons and daughters. Big bull elephants live alone and join the females at mating time.

Soccer News

AYSO meeting

Parents are invited to the Tiger soccer meeting:
Tue. March 23
 7:30 p.m.
 M. Kessler's house
 1234 Royal Pl. 543-9876

Team Tiger

This year the Tigers have won 3 games. Steve Sloan. the goalie. has stopped 4 goals with his head. Greg Kessler has scored 1 goal and Tom Brown 2 goals.

HOLIDAY POSTCARDS

Level: Intermediate–Challenging

Subject Areas: Language Arts, Art, History

InfoNet: A unique way to create your own greeting cards is by using the Postcard project. You create a front graphic scene and then on the back write your greeting. The cards are printed four to a page. For this example you will be making a Christmas greeting.

This Project: Students create their own holiday greeting cards in a postcard format. They design the front of the card and write a greeting on the back. The cards are put through the printer twice for a very professional appearance.

HOLIDAY POSTCARDS
STUDENT GUIDE

1. Open the Post Card project from the main menu and choose Wide Orientation.

2. Select a Landscape Backdrop design that you like from the Backdrop screen. Click OK.

3. You now have a screen that shows a page that is ready for you to create your project.

4. To write text on the front of the card, select the Text tool from the Object menu and draw a text box in the white area of the screen.

5. Now type in the text.

6. If the size of the font is too large, highlight and choose Size from the Text menu. Select a smaller size and write your text.

7. Let's add a border for the front. Select the Object icon from the Tool Palette and choose Border. You now have a greyed-out area around the page. Double-click on the grey area and choose a border.

8. To access the back of the card, select Project and choose Back of PostCard.

9. Choose No Layout from the Landscape Layout screen.

10. You now have a blank area on which to write your text. Select the Text tool and make a text box on the left side of the card. The address to which you are sending the card goes on the right side. If you have room in your text space, you might want to add a graphic.

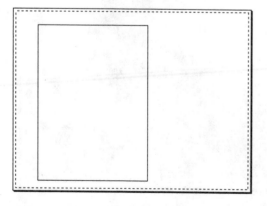

11. When you are ready to print, select Print from the File menu and print your work.

12. When you select Print from the File menu, you will then be printing the front of the card.

13. After your postcard front comes out of the printer, turn the paper over and reinsert it into the printer so that the second side is printed. If you are using cardstock for your card, print the card on regular paper to make sure you are turning it over correctly. The card prints 4 to a page with crosshairs in the center of the paper to guide you in cutting.

What Else Can I Do?

- Make postcards greetings for Easter, graduation, Thanksgiving, Halloween, Mother's Day, Father's Day, special school events, invitations, etc.

PERSONALIZED STUDY CARDS

Level: Intermediate–Challenging

Subject Areas: Language Arts, Art, History, Math

InfoNet: Using study cards for learning facts that you need to memorize is a helpful tool. The cards print out eight to a page and then you cut them apart. Write whatever facts you need on the blank side. This project gives you your very own set of cards.

This Project: Students create their own sets of study cards for use in their studies. The front of each card has a picture with the students name on it. When it prints out, the students then writes the facts to study on the back. Anything could be written on the back: multiplication facts, states and capitals, chemistry elements, spelling words, etc.

Michael Smith
Oakview School

PERSONALIZED STUDY CARDS
STUDENT GUIDE

1. Open the Business Card project from the main menu and choose Wide Orientation.

2. Choose a Backdrop design that you like from the Backdrop screen.

3. The next screen is where you choose the layout or the way the card is designed. For this project, choose a layout and press OK.

4. You now have a screen that shows a page that is ready for you to create your project. You have spaces for text, and the graphics are already there.

5. Let's type in the text first. Double-click on the Text placeholder and type in your text. You might want to have your name and then your school' s name.

6. If the size of the font is too large, highlight and choose Size from the Text menu. Select a smaller size and write your text.

7. Let's add a border for the text. Select the Object icon from the Tool Palette and choose Border. You now have a greyed-out area around the page. Double-click on the grey area and choose a border for text on the screen.

8. When you are ready to print, select Print from the File menu and print your work.

What Else Can I Do?

- Make playing cards for a game.
- Make cards for your younger brother or sister to learn math facts.

Rosa Mills
Park School

ILLUSTRATED INFORMATION CARDS

Level: Intermediate–Challenging

Subject Areas: Language Arts, Art

InfoNet: As you study different cultures, you learn about unique customs that belong to those cultures. In this project, you create folded cards that illustrate and tell about some aspect of the culture or custom about which you are studying. For this particular project you will be making an informational folded card about the Chinese New Year.

This Project: As your class studies various cultures throughout the world, have them create illustrated information cards for display on the bulletin board or as part of their assigned reports.

You will need to model the following instructions for the students before they begin.

ILLUSTRATED INFORMATION CARDS STUDENT GUIDE

1. Open the Greeting Card project from the main menu and choose Top Fold.

2. Choose Dragon from the Portrait Backdrop screen. Click OK.

3. The next screen is where you choose the layout or the way the letter is designed. For this project, choose No Layout and press OK.

4. You now have a screen that shows a page that has a picture of a dragon on it, and you are ready to write some text.

5. Select the Text tool from the Tool Palette. Move your mouse over to the page, click at the top left-hand corner and drag diagonally to make an area where you can write a title for your card.

6. Now you need to go to the inside of the card. Select Project from the menu bar and choose Inside of Card. Choose Blank Page. Click OK. Now choose No Layout from the next screen. Click OK.

7. Repeat Step 5 here.

8. You see a cursor in the upper left-hand corner. Type in your story. Be sure to keep your story in the text box. If it goes outside of the box, it will not print.

If it does not fit, highlight the text and choose a smaller size from the Text menu.

9. To add a graphic to your story, select the Object icon form the Tool Palette, select a Square Graphic and double-click on the placeholder when it appears. For this project, you can find the firecracker graphics in Holiday 1(CD-ROM) by changing libraries. You can move the graphic to the correct area by placing the mouse arrow on it and dragging to the new location.

10. Let's add a border for the text. Select the Object icon from the Tool Palette and choose Border. You now have a greyed-out area around the page. Double-click on the grey area and choose a border for text on the screen.

11. When you are ready to print, select Print from the File menu and print your work.

What Else Can I Do?

- Write illustrated information cards telling about seahorses.
- Make a card telling about Hanukkah, etc.

Hanukkah
A Festival of Lights

Jewish people throughout the world celebrate Hanukkah in December. They light eight candles, one for each night. They play a spinning top game with a dreidle. Hanukkah celebrates the rededication of the temple in Jerusalem.

CONVERSATIONS

Level: Intermediate–Challenging

Subject Areas: Language Arts, Art, History

InfoNet: Imagine the meeting of two figures from the past. What do you think that they might say to each other? In this project you have a chance to use your imagination to have two historical characters speak to each other. In this example Washington and Lincoln are meeting.

This Project: Students will be able to synthesize their studies of various historical figures by creating a conversation between two of them. Using graphics and the Sign project, students write imaginary conversations. These conversations are not limited to humans but could also take place between many different objects ranging from foods to clothing.

You will need to model the following instructions for the students before they begin.

CONVERSATIONS STUDENT GUIDE

1. Open the Sign project from the main menu and choose Wide Orientation.

2. Choose Blank Page from the Backdrop screen.

3. The next screen is where you choose the layout or the way the sign is designed. For this project, choose No Layout and press OK.

4. You now have a screen that shows a blank page and is ready for you to create your project.

5. Let's first input the graphics for the page. Select the Object tool from the Tool Palette and select square graphic. Move the Placeholder to where you want the first of your graphics. Double-click on the graphic and choose your graphic. You probably will have to change Graphics Libraries. Click on the Change Libraries button and search for your graphic. The ones in this example are from Holiday Collection 6 and Holiday Collection 2.

6. Now that your two graphics are placed, let's place speech bubbles next to them. Select Square Graphic from the Object menu and double-click on the placeholder.

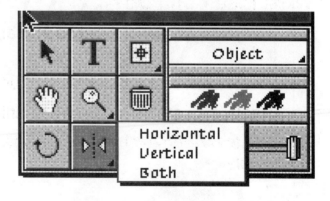

You can find the speech bubbles in PSD Accessories. Place the speech bubbles next to each president. If you need to change the direction of the bubble, highlight the bubble by clicking on it once and then click on the Flip tool in the Tool Palette. Choose Horizontal.

7. Select the Text Tool from the Tool Palette. Move your mouse over to the corner of the speech bubble and drag diagonally to make an area where you can write the text.

8. If the size of the font is too large, highlight and choose Size from the Text menu. Select a smaller size and write your text.

9. Let's add a border for the text. Select the Object icon from the Tool Palette and choose Border. You now have a greyed-out area around the page. Double-click on the grey area and choose a border for text on the screen.

10. When you are ready to print, select Print from the File menu and print your work.

What Else Can I Do?

- Create conversations between Martin Luther King and a child.

- Create conversations between fruits and vegetables.

- Create conversations between animals.

- Create conversations between various professional people.

IMPORTANT PEOPLE IN OUR LIVES

Level: Intermediate–Challenging

Subject Area: Language Arts and Technology

InfoNet: It takes many personnel to keep a school site running smoothly. The people who work at the site often work quietly behind the scenes. This project lets them become more visible as significant people and informs us of their work and the skills needed to perform it.

This Project: Students interview the personnel who work at the school site to provid a safe and educational environment. They take notes of the interview either by hand, using a tape recorder, or, if available, with a laptop computer. This is done individually or in cooperative groups. After the interviews are completed, students use the Sign project to write and publish the interview.

Ms. Lopez
Our Librarian

Ms. Lopez has been at our school for three years. She speaks Spanish and English.
She has two girls and a husband. Her girls attend our school.

IMPORTANT PEOPLE IN OUR LIVES STUDENT GUIDE

1. Open Sign from the project menu. Select the Tall option.

2. Select Blank Page from the Portrait Backdrop menu and click OK.

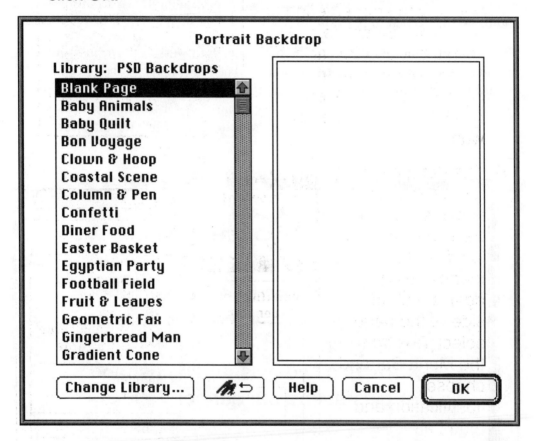

3. Select Sign 11 and click OK. This particular layout gives you placeholders for Headline, Square Graphic, and Text. You might want to choose a different layout later as you learn the various types.

4. Double-click on the Text Placeholder. You can now input your text by typing in the text area. If you have a lot of text to enter, you might want to change the font size before you start entering your text. Select Text from the Menu Bar at the top of the screen, choose size, and then choose the font size you want.

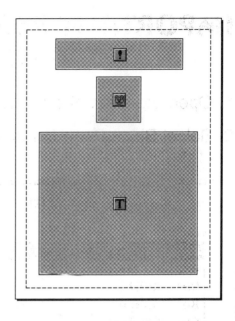

5. The default setting for the Text block is centered. To have your text left justified, that means fitting against the left side of the page, select Text from the Menu Bar and choose Justification and then Left.

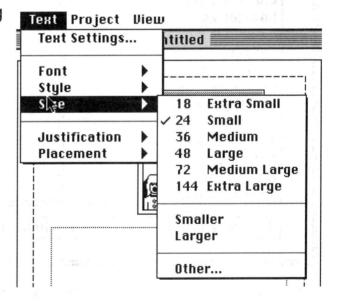

6. Type in the information that you have from the interview. If your version of *The Print Shop* has a spell check, use it when you are finished writing.

7. Now it is time to place a graphic in your report. Double-click on the Square Graphic placeholder. You now have a dialog screen where you can choose a graphic. Click on a graphic choice and click OK. You can change the graphic at any time by double-clicking on it and repeating the choosing procedure.

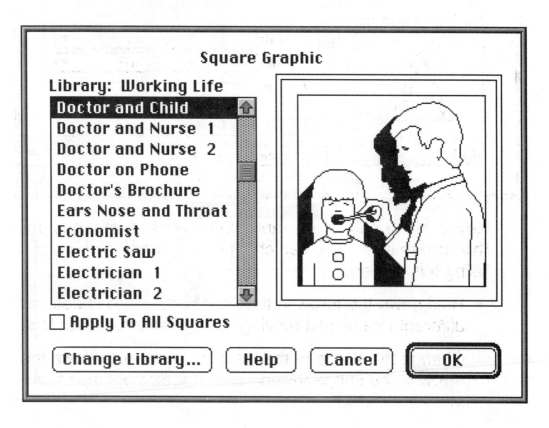

8. Now let's choose a Headline. Double-click on the Headline placeholder. You are taken to a Headline Text screen.

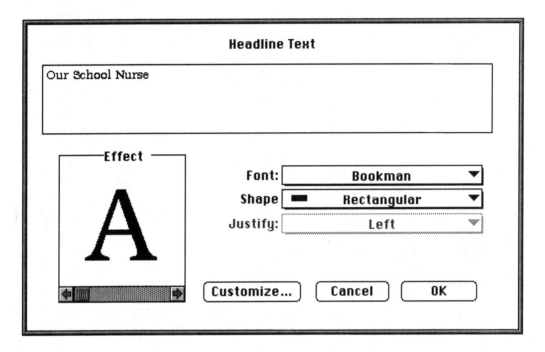

Key in the text that you want. You can make changes from this screen also. You can change font, shape, and color using this screen.

- Hold down the arrow in the Font section and choose a different font by just moving the mouse arrow over to it.

- Change the shape of the Headline by holding down the arrow in the shape section and choosing a shape from the ones shown.

- To change the color of the Headline, click on Customize and select a color from the choices given. Click OK.

9. To place a border around your document, select Object from the Tool Palette menu and move your mouse arrow to Border. A grey border appears around the document. Double-click in the grey border area, and you can choose your border from the ones shown on the screen. Click OK, and the border appears around your document. If you don't like it, you can double-click again and choose a new border.

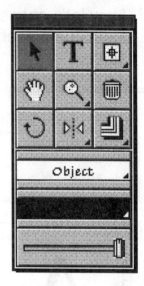

10. To print your document, select Print from the File menu.

What Else Can I Do?

- Ask the teacher to put all of the interviews together into a class book.

- Make a certificate for the person you interviewed using the Certificate project from *The Print Shop*.

- Interview people in the community and use the computer to create and publish your project.

Hints: If the writing disappears as you get to the bottom of your page, you need to highlight the writing and choose a smaller font size. Highlight the text by holding down the mouse button and moving over the text until it is dark.

Ms. Brooks
Our Police Officer

Whenever there is a problem, Ms. Brooks likes to help solve it. She has wanted to be a police officer since she was in the second grade. Sometimes her mother worries about her. Ms. Brooks says that her belt and everything that she wears is very heavy.

Our School Nurse

Mr. Hamer is our school nurse. He is at our school Monday, Wednesday and Thursday. When he is at our school he helps us when we get hurt. When new students come to our school, the health record is checked and the student is weighed and measured . Every two years he checks our eyes. Mr Hamer says that it is very important to wear your glasses if you need them.

Mr Hamer learned to be a nurse when he was in the Army. He had gone to U.C.L.A. first.

WISH YOU WERE HERE!

Level: Intermediate–Challenging

Subject Areas: Language Arts, Social Science

InfoNet: Each place that you visit has some unique feature. It could be an architecturally unique building, strange animals that are only found in that area, or geographic phenomena.

This Project: With the students, decide on which areas of the globe they are going to research as background for a trip they are planning. This research can be done individually or in small groups. If the appropriate technology is available, use some of the CD-ROMs that contain atlases, or other appropriate reference materials. After the research, students or groups draft a postcard that would be sent from a place along the route that they are taking for their trip. The information that they have found in their research is used in designing the front of the postcard and in composing the text they write on the back of the card.

Student Preparation: Research a location that you would like to visit. Note the uniqueness of the location. What are the features that you will remember for many years? You are going to design a postcard that can be sent from the location. The front of the card shows graphically something about the place. The back of the card is written as if you are describing your location to a friend. Draft a design for the front of your postcard. Draft the text for the back. (See page 268.)

DESIGN YOUR POSTCARD

Front

Back

WISH YOU WERE HERE! STUDENT GUIDE

1. Select Post Card project from the main menu.

2. Choose Wide or Tall Layout and choose Blank Page.

3. Choose the No Layout choice from the next menu.

4. To add graphics to the design of the postcard front, you can use Square Graphics, Column Graphics, or Row Graphics. Each of these choices can be changed in size.

Adding a Square Graphic to the postcard:

- Select the Object icon from the Tool menu.

- Choose the Square Graphic selection. When you do this a placeholder for the Square Graphic appears on the screen. Move the placeholder to where you want the graphic. To do this, hold down the mouse button inside the placeholder and just move the graphic.

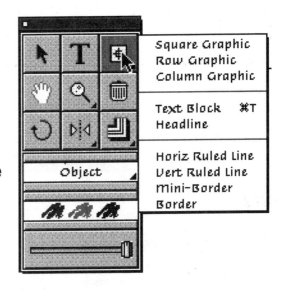

5. Double-click on the graphic placeholder and select a graphic. If you need a graphic that is not listed on the screen, select Change Library and search for an appropriate graphic.

6. Graphic Options:

   • Adding column graphics or row graphics to your design: Follow the directions above and choose Column or Row graphics instead of Square Graphic.

   • Adding a border to your design: Select Object from the Menu Bar or use the Object icon in the Tool Menu. Choose Border. When you do that a grey border appears around your postcard. Double-click on that grey border and choose the border you want.

7. To go to the back of the card, select Project from the Menu Bar and choose Back of Card.

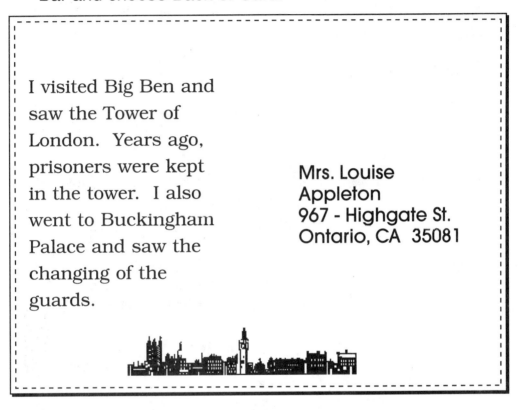

I visited Big Ben and saw the Tower of London. Years ago, prisoners were kept in the tower. I also went to Buckingham Palace and saw the changing of the guards.

Mrs. Louise Appleton
967 - Highgate St.
Ontario, CA 35081

8. To choose a layout for the back of the card, select Change Layout from the Project menu on the Menu Bar. Choose a layout that you like. Remember that you need a text space for the address and a text space for the message. You might like to use Postcard #9.

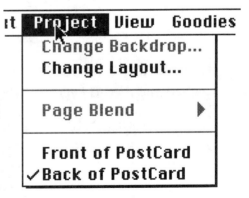

9. Double-click in the text placeholder to begin writing your text. If the size of the font is too large for what you want to write, select the Text menu from the Menu Bar, choose the size option, and then choose the size text you want.

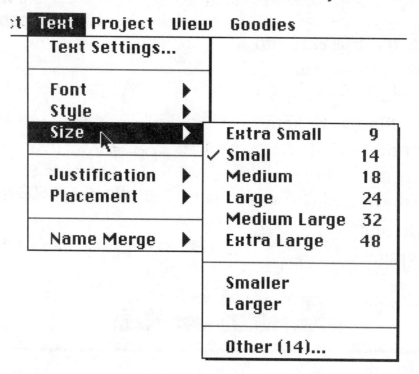

10. Write your message describing your location.

11. To write the address, double-click on the text placeholder on the right and type in the address.

12. To print your postcard, you need to print one side at a time and put the paper through the printer twice.

- Select File and choose Print. Click Front or Back on the Print dialog screen and then click Print.

- After the side is printed, feed the paper back into the printer so it can print the other side. You might want to do a test on plain paper before using heavier paper for the post card.

What Else Can I Do?

- Create a postcard as if written from a fictional character.

- Create a postcard to remind someone of a special event such as your birthday.

- Ask your teacher to put all the postcards on the bulletin board for a display.

- During school vacations, collect information about the places you visit. Design postcards using the information.

- Create postcards as if they were sent by historical figures.

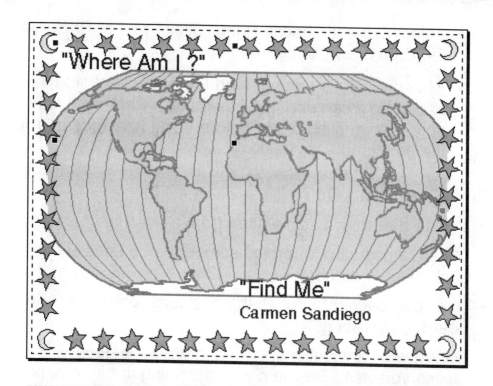

"Where Am I ?"

"Find Me"

Carmen Sandiego

You who think you are so clever, have one week to find me. Here is a clue: I am near Mt.Olympus. You might find me eating olives.

Carmen

Mr Columbo
345 - Convertable st.
Hollywood CA. 97564

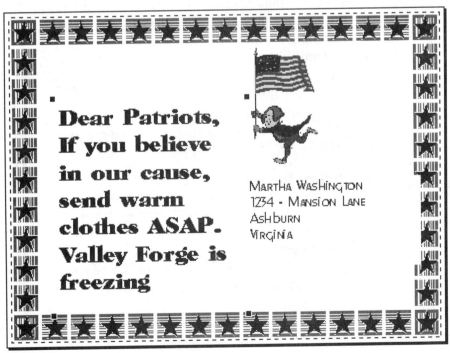

LEARNING KEYBOARDING SKILLS

It will be important that your students have keyboarding skills as they work on their *Print Shop* projects. This will allow them to work more creatively on the computer, rather than spending their time locating keys and deciding how to use them. On pages eight and nine you will find some ideas for transition-time or sponge activities which build keyboarding skills, as well as reproductions of Macintosh and IBM keyboards for your use.

This Project

With the prevalence of computers in both the classroom and home, there is a definite need for young students to become familiar with the keyboard. As students begin using computers more and more for writing their own stories, they may at times lose their flow of writing while searching for the correct keys. Familiarizing young students with the keyboard will help to alleviate the hunt-and-peck method and lead to a smoother writing activity. To address this need, you will find a graphic of a Macintosh keyboard as well as an IBM keyboard on pages 279 and 280 and some classroom suggestions for keyboarding activities on pages 278 and 279.

Before Beginning

- Using a keyboard, demonstrate to your students the correct positions on the home row and how those fingers remain on the home row even when reaching for letters above or below the home row. Have your students color in the home row of keys so they stand out.

- Show your students how the thumb is used to press the space bar.

- Duplicate the keyboard blackline masters found on pages 279 and 280 at an enlargement of 150%. Then you can either laminate them or slip them into plastic sleeves and keep them at students' desks.

Keyboarding Activities

Using one of the keyboards on pages 279 and 280, the following activities can be used as transition-time activities in your classroom—those three minutes before recess and after math, before going to lunch, or even before the end of the day.

- Make a list of the week's spelling words either on the board or on an overhead. Then have your students practice typing each word.

- Have your students practice locating special keys on the keyboard (e.g., tab, space bar, return, shift, delete, etc.).

- Write a math problem on the board and have your students type in the numbers to match the problem.

- Have your students practice writing their friends' names, using the shift key for capital letters.

- Write a letter on the board and have your students find that letter on their keyboards.

- You might want to choose a special word of the day and have your students practice typing it.

- Have your students practice typing holiday names. The capital letters are good practice for using the shift key.

- Write the day and date on the board and have your students type them on their keyboards.

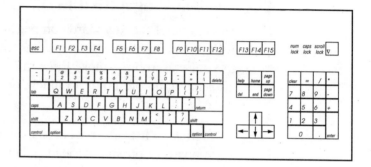

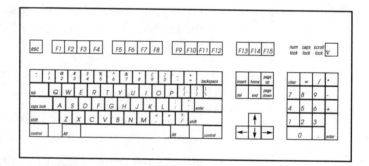

Mac Keyboard

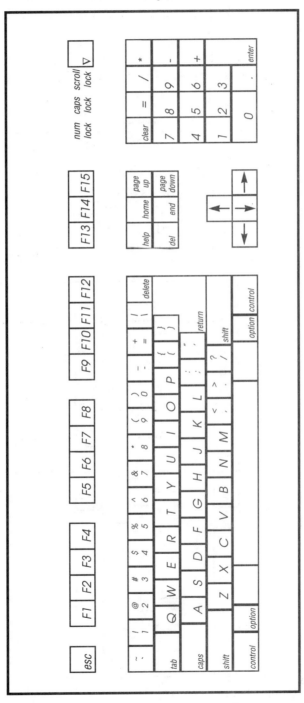

IBM and PC Compatible Keyboard

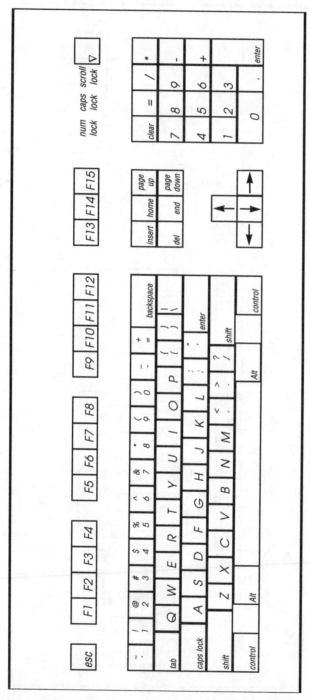

GLOSSARY

Adapter—electronic piece that adapts to a device so a computer can control the device.

After Dark—a utility from Berkeley Systems called a screen saver.

AppleTalk—the AppleTalk network is how your Mac talks to your laser printer, other Macs, or other machines. All these machines need to be hooked up in order to talk.

Application—a computer software program you use.

Bar Code—grouping of thin lines which when accessed by an electronic bar-code reader, reveal information.

Baud (baud rate)—speed at which a modem can send information.

Bit—short for binary digit. One bit is the smallest unit of information that the computer can work with.

Bulletin Board Service—service usually set up by an online organization to provide or exchange information.

Bundling—usually, the practice of selling hardware (e.g., a computer) and including free one or more pieces of software.

Button—electronic item on a computer screen that is "pushed" in order for something to happen.

Byte—a byte is eight bits strung together. Most computer information is organized into bytes.

CD-ROM—compact disk read-only memory. A disk which holds up to 600 megabytes of information.

CD-ROM Player—disk drive which allows the CD-ROM to be played.

Clip Art—artwork that is electronically cut and pasted onto other documents.

CPU—central processing unit. The "brains" of a computer. Often a tiny microprocessor chip which runs the entire system.

Crash—what happens when your computer stops working suddenly or the system breaks down. (A very bad deal!)

Cursor—little mark indicating your position on the screen. It sometimes blinks on and off and will move when you move the mouse or press certain keys.

Database—collection of information stored in computerized form.

Default—any time an automatic decision is already made for you by the computer or software program.

Desktop—background on your screen when you are using a Macintosh or other windows-like program.

Desktop Publishing—process of creating printed documents that look professionally produced.

Dialog Box—a box or window on the screen that you can "dialog" with and make choices from.

Digital—information represented by numbers.

Digital Camera—outputs images in digital form instead of regular photographic film.

Disk—thin, circular, or rectangular object used to store computer data.

Disk Drive—part of the computer where the disk goes.

DOS—disk operating systems. Many types of computers have systems called DOS. Usually refers to IBM PC or other compatible computers.

D

Download—to receive information (like a file) from another computer to yours through the modem. Or you may take a copy of a document from a disk and download it onto your computer.

Drag—use the mouse to position the pointer over an object, press and hold the mouse button and move the mouse, thereby moving the object to another position on the screen.

E

E-mail—short for electronic mail you can send or receive directly on your computer via modem.

Ethernet—a local area network connecting computers together with cables so the computers can share the same information.

F

Fiber Optics—a communications system that uses dozens of hair-thin strands of glass that move information at the speed of light.

Font—a complete set of type of one size and style.

G

Graphic—an electronic picture.

H

Hacker—computer enthusiast who is willing to "hack" away at understanding the computer for long periods of time.

Hardware—parts of the computer which are external (modem, printer, hard drive, keyboard).

I

IBM (International Business Machines)—an international computer company.

Icons—little pictures on the screen which represent files of other computer applications.

I

Import—to bring information from one document or computer screen into another document.

Interactive—program, game, or presentation where the user has some control over what is going on.

Interface—connection between two items so they can work together.

Internet—worldwide network of about half a million computers belonging to research organizations, the military, institutions of learning, corporations, and so on.

K

K, KB (Kilobyte)—a unit for measuring the size of things on hard disks or computer applications. It represents the memory of an item. One kilobyte is equal to 1,024 bytes.

Keyboard—piece of hardware that has keys like a typewriter.

L

Laptop Computer—a computer small enough to fit on your lap. Runs on batteries and is portable.

Laserdisc—also known as videodisc, similar to a music CD, but it also holds visual images. Information can be accessed by remote control or bar code.

Laserdisc Player—machine which plays the laserdisc.

Laser Printer—printer which produces documents that look professionally printed.

LCD Panel—a device which fits over the overhead projector and when connected to a computer will project whatever is on the computer screen onto a large viewing screen. LCD means liquid crystal display. A liquid compound is wedged between two grids of electrodes to create an image.

Macintosh—name of an Apple computer which was the first computer to use the windows and mouse formats.

Mb, MB (Megabyte)—short for a unit of measure measuring the size of electronic items (like files and documents). One megabyte is equal to 1,048,567 bytes of memory.

Memory—temporary storage space in your computer as opposed to the permanent storage space on the hard disk. Think of the hard disk as a filing cabinet where everything is stored. Memory is your desk while you are temporarily working on the items inside the filing cabinet.

Menu—a displayed list of commands or options from which you can choose.

Modem—device that allows computers to communicate with other computers via the telephone line.

Monitor—another word for the computer screen.

Mouse—small device connected to the keyboard which you move across the top of your desk to manipulate the pointer or cursor on the screen.

Mouse Pad—a small pad on which you can roll your mouse around. Designed to give you a better grip than a desktop.

MS-DOS (Microsoft Disk Operating System)—this is the most commonly used system for IBM PCs and other compatible computers.

Multimedia—a computer presentation that involves still images, moving video, sound, animation, art, or a combination of all the above.

Network—communication or connection system that lets your computer talk with another computer, printer, hard disk, or other device.

Online—communicating with other computers through your modem or network.

P

Paint Program—software application that provides electronic versions of paintbrushes, paint cans, eraser, pencils, scissors, etc., in order to create illustrations.

PC (Personal Computer)—designed to be used by an individual person.

Port—a socket usually found on the back of hardware where a cable is connected.

PowerBook—Apple's laptop computer.

Printer—device that takes the text and images sent from the computer and presents them on paper.

Prompt—a symbol or question on the screen that "prompts" you to take action and tell the computer what to do next.

Q

QuickTime—software product from Apple that is loaded onto your computer so you can run movies. It requires a great deal of space.

R

RAM (Random Access Memory)—electronic circuits in your computer which hold information. It is the temporary memory used while the computer is turned on. You will need to save any work you do onto a disk or a file on the hard drive. Otherwise, your work will be lost when the computer is shut off. RAM is referred to as volatile because the contents disappear when the computer is turned off.

ROM (Read-Only Memory)—information stored on ROM remains intact. The information is usually programmed right onto the chip or disk and cannot be altered or added to. That is why it is called read-only.

S

Scanner—device that takes a picture of an image that exists outside the computer and digitizes the image to put it on the computer.

S

Screen Saver—a software application that blanks the screen and replaces the screen with a nonharmful picture. By moving the mouse or touching a key, the screen saver shuts off, and your original screen automatically comes back up. If you leave your computer on for a long time, the image can burn onto the screen.

Software—instructions for the computer which are stored on a disk. These disks must be loaded onto the hard drive of the computer so that the computer will know what to do. Some software applications are already loaded onto the computer.

Spreadsheet Program—software program for financial or other number-related information processing. A spreadsheet is composed of rows and columns with individual boxes (cells) inside of each to hold information.

T

Telecommunications—communications carried on from one computer to another through the telephone line and modem.

Terminal—a screen and keyboard along with any circuits necessary to connect it to a main computer.

Toolbox—many software applications, especially ones with paint options, come with a toolbox which appears on the screen in the form of a palette.

U

Upgrade—to choose newer, more powerful packages (hard or software).

Upload—using a modem, you put one of your files onto a network (or online service) and load the file onto the service so other people have access to it.

Utility—a software program that is not used to create something (like an application) but rather it is used to enhance your working environment. *After Dark* is a utility for your computer system.

Videodisc—see laserdisc.

Virus—a software program designed to destroy data on your computer or corrupt your system software. Some viruses are so destructive, they can wipe out entire disks. Viruses are created illegally and can travel from computer to computer through disks, networks, and modems. Using virus detection software is a safe way to protect your system.

Virtual Reality—a simulated environment which appears to be real through use of a computer.

Window—rectangular frame on the screen in which you see and work with a particular software application.

Word Processor—software applications that allow you to type documents with a variety of tools to make work time easier and more efficient.